RURAL PRESS
PROBLEMS AND PROSPECTS

V.S. Gupta, presently Professor at the Haryana Agricultural University, had earlier worked in several media related positions in the University: Editor, Head of the Farm Information and Communication Service and the Public Relations Office. He was awarded the UNDP Fellowship for training in Europe and was selected for the Journalist Fellowship Award for working in the area of Environment and Development.

Prof. Gupta has contributed a number of papers in seminars, conferences, Journals and Newspapers in India and abroad. In collaboration with Ranjit Singh, he had edited *Communication Planning for Socio-Economic Development* (1994) and with M. R. Dua, *Media and Development* (1994). His latest publication. *Third Revolution in Indian Perspective: Contemporary Issues and Themes in Communication* (1995) is published by Concept.

The books and monographs have been acclaimed in the national press and academic journals. He is associated with academic programmes in journalism and mass communication at the post-graduate level of several universities in the country. He represents AMIC as its Zonal Representative in North India.

Rajeshwar Dyal, has an experience of 18 years in communication research, training, development of training material, interaction with national and international media organisations and activists. Presently, he is working as Media Advisor with Friedrich Ebert Foundation, which aims at democratisation and pluralism in media, organising media activities with media in the government and private sector, academia from various departments and other research institutions. He was with the Indian Institute of Mass Communication, New Delhi for 15 years prior to his joining the present asignment in 1992.

RURAL PRESS
PROBLEMS AND PROSPECTS

Proceedings of the seminars organised at Jaipur, Dhenkanal and Madras during 1994

Edited by

V. S. GUPTA
Professor
Directorate of Publications
Haryana Agricultural University,
Hisar

RAJESHWAR DYAL
Media Advisor
Friedrich Ebert Stiftung
New Delhi

FRIEDRICH EBERT STIFTUNG
AMIC

CONCEPT PUBLISHING COMPANY, NEW DELHI 110059

ISBN 81-7022-573-6

First Published 1995

Published and printed by
Ashok Kumar Mittal
Concept Publishing Company
A/15-16, Commercial Block, Mohan Garden,
NEW DELHI - 110 059
Phones : 5554042, 5504042

FOREWORD

AMIC's interest in the rurul and community press goes back more than two decades. A seminar on rural communication was held in 1973. A study of the provincial press in Malaysia and the Philippines was published in 1974. And an AMIC Seminar Group on Rural Press in Asia had this to say in 1976: One of the great problems in the sphere of rural literacy is the availability of follow up reading material. The rural newspaper provides the opportunity and motivation for reading and will, in due course, reinforce and supplement efforts made in class rooms and establish the reading habit. In addition, it brings development information, as well as news which helps improve agriculture, health, sanitation and civic conditions. Any system which promotes the early establishment and growth of the rural press in provincial centres and townships, makes an important contribution to the speed of national development.

One of the many studies undertaken by AMIC was a study of community newspapers in Asia. From India, *Rajsthan Patrika* figured prominently as one of the five newspapers from all over Asia. In the above study, the story of growth and development of *Rajasthan Patrika* makes fascinating reading.

It was, therefore, in the fitness of things that AMIC–India, as a part of its in-country activities, organized a series of three seminars on Role and Development of Rural Press during 1994.

I am glad to know that the papers presented at the three seminars have focused on specific aspects of the Role and Development of Rural Press.

On behalf of AMIC, I would like to convey my appreciation to the members of the organizing committees of these seminars, the resource persons and the participants for the time and effort they have invested to ensure the success of these seminars. I would also like to record my appreciation of their collective effort in bringing out this publication, based on the papers presented at the seminars. I hope this publication will further help in promoting development of Rural Press in the country.

Vijay Menon
Secretary-General
Asian Mass Communication
Research and Information Centre,
Singapore

19 June 1995

INTRODUCTION

Rural Press constitutes one of the most important media for reaching out to the hundreds of million people in all parts of the country. As a link between the policy makers, development bureaucracy and farmers; as a second line of conversion of scientific knowledge into information for utilisation in the field situation, imparting adult education and also for reinforcing literacy habit, Rural Press is being increasingly recognised as a viable means for the promotion of social awareness and development. It is a promising medium for disseminating information and knowledge about nutrition, health and hygiene, improved farm practices, family planning measures and development plans to those sections of society where the information is needed most.

During the last more than two decades several organizations such as UNESCO, IPDÇ and AMIC have been paying special attention towards the problems, prospects and development of the Rural Press.

AMIC's interest in rural and community press goes back to more than two decades. AMIC has believed that growth of Rural Press in provincial centres and townships makes an important contribution to the speed of national development. One of the many studies undertaken by AMIC was a study of community newspapers in Asia. From India, *Rajasthan Patrika* figured prominently as one of the five newspapers from all over Asia. In the above study, the story of growth and development of *Rajasthan Patrika* makes fascinating reading.

In November 1986, AMIC had organized a three-day Workshop at Singapore on Rural Press Development in Asia. The Workshop, which was sponsored by the Communication Assistance Foundation, was designed as a major forum to review the development of the Rural Press in Asia. The underlying objective was to look at various success sources to see if they could be replicated in other countries. The participants at the Workshop, in which representatives from 11 countries participated, felt that the Rural Press could serve as a voice of the masses and thereby help them be treated as full-fledged citizens rather than as second class citizens. It was felt that one of the primary objectives of the Rural Press should be to create consciousness among rural leaders. In the long run this could motivate the rural population to take an active part in the development processes. The Friedrich Ebert Stiftung and the West German Government have been actively associated with UNESCO in encouraging rural newspapers in several countries in Africa. One of the Communication Manuals—the Layman Printer by Frank Barton and Gunter Lehrke had highlighted some of the rural press projects in Africa.

Keeping in view the fact that in India Rural Press constitutes an important segment of the media situation, AMIC-India, with support from FES, decided to organize a series of three seminars in the country during 1994—Jaipur, 21-23 April; Dhenkanal, 22-23 October and Madras, 2-3 December. These seminars provided a suitable opportunity to the participants, AMIC members, media practitioners to deliberate on various aspects of the Rural Press development. The papers presented at the seminars touched upon different aspects of the problems and prospects of the Rural Press in the country. The participants brought their varied and rich experience to bear upon the discussion on some of the critical issues through these papers. These papers have been put together in this publication for wider dissemination and to be of use for reference and consultation by the students and teachers of journalism, media practitioners and all others interested in the Rural Press development. It has not been possible to take all the papers presented at the seminar, only some of the selected ones have been used in this publication for wider public discussion and dissemination.

We take this opportunity of expressing our deep gratitude to every single participant and observer, chairman and rapporteurs of various sessions, members of the local coordinating committee and authorities of various institutions who had collaborated in holding these seminars. We would particularly like to place on record our deep gratitude to Mr. K. P. Singh Deo, Union Minister for Information and Broadcasting; Dr. J. S. Yadava, Director, Indian Institute of Mass Communication; Padamshri Prof. A. K. Banerji, Emeritus Fellow, UGC; Sh. G. P. Jain, Veteran Journalist; Sh. K. S. Ramakrishnan, Director, Research Institute for Newspapers Development; Dr. Sanjeev Bhanawat, Incharge, Centre for Mass Communication, University of Rajasthan; Dr. Manohar Prabhakar; Dr. K. R. Singh, President, Public Relations Society of India; Sh. Gulab Kothari, Managing Director, *Rajasthan Patrika;* Prof. M. R. Dua and our colleagues in AMIC—Mr. Ashok Panda and Mr. R. V. Rajan.

We hope that the papers presented at these seminars, which we have included in this book, will go a long way in encouraging the development and growth of Rural Press in the country.

We also place on record our gratitude to Friedrich Ebert Stiftung for sponsoring the three seminars and support for bringing out the proceedings of the seminars.

V. S. Gupta
Zonal Representative
AMIC

Rajeshwar Dyal
Media Advisor
FES

CONTENTS

CONTENTS

1

ROLE AND DEVELOPMENT OF RURAL PRESS IN INDIA

— J. S. Yadava

The history and growth of the Press in India coincided with early reformation and liberation struggle of modern times. The first newspaper in India was published in 1780. It was in English. Since then, despite inhibiting factors like low literacy and poor purchasing power, the Press in India has come a long way.

The total number of newspapers and journals at the end of 1991 was 30214 published in 93 languages. Of these, 3229 were dailies. As per the latest figure available, the combined circulation is 58.8 million. Newspapers published in Hindi had the highest circulation of 20.2 million followed by English at 7.3 million.

The Press in India, on the whole, concentrates on political events, controversies and personalities. Crime and entertainment in urban areas also find fair coverage. It is no secret that our press is largely urban and elitist and bypass the multitude of people who live in rural and tribal India. Reporting from rural areas and about rural people is far and between, that too when some politician goes for inauguration, foundation stone laying ceremonies or for an aerial view of the flood affected areas. A genuine and powerful rural press is yet to emerge in India.

Some people tend to equate rural press with what could be best described as farm journals/magazines and small newspapers. Such a view is erroneous. It is true there are about 300 farm periodicals published in India. They provide detailed and specific information about agriculture and other related activities. However, being specialised publication, their circulation is usually small and is mostly confined to the concerned officials, professionals and well-to-do farmers. As such, their impact is limited as far as the majority of people living in rural areas are concerned.

The small newspapers with a circulation of less than 15,000 are also not really rural newspapers. Most of these small newspapers are not only irregular in publication but their contents are also often bordering on yellow journalism. They write against some officials or businessmen to get some financial support or patronage either by pleasing or black-mailing them. The readership which is usually very small is also confined to some official circles and others in the towns of their publications. These small newspapers neither have any reading material of interest for rural people nor reach them. Not that all small newspapers fit into dismal description. Some are dedicated and making noble efforts. But this was the broad picture that emerged after a survey of district level newspapers in two states of India, UP and Karnataka.

Instead, some of the high circulation newspapers seem to be doing better, both in terms of contents and reach to the rural areas. In Kerala, Tamil Nadu and Andhra Pradesh, newspapers have reasonable circulation in rural areas. Kerala has fairly high literacy, 89.81 per cent. Even in rural-urban distinction in human settlements are not that mark in the south, being all the dispersed type, as opposed to the nucleated one in the north. Kerala, with the population of about 29 million (3.4 per cent of India's total population) has the distinction of accounting for about 10.3 per cent of the total circulation of the country with a share of over 5.5 million copies. Ever rising circulation graph of the Telugu daily, *Eenadu*, in recent years is the result of its going 'local' both in contents and idioms. It is reaching almost most of the villages in Andhra Pradesh.

As we all know, press is essential and an integral part of democratic functioning of governance of any society. The same is true of India also. The press as an institution gathers, processes and disseminates information that keeps the nation going. While democratic activities and functionings are robust in all sections of Indian society and more so in the rural India, the press which supposed to provide essential inputs and links to healthy democratic functionings is largely confined to elite in urban areas. This perhaps is one of the causes of some of the aberrations and malfunctionings that we witness in functioning of our democratic institutions. Like many other sectors of our economy and social life, the development and growth of press is also skewed in favour of urban population.

It is true that the press has come a long way in becoming professional in its approach and showing excellence in production and is doing very well in performing the traditional watch dog function. But it has to a great extent failed to pay adequate attention to some cardinal objectives of newspapers as envisaged by Mahatma Gandhi which are still relevant to the healthy functioning and operation of the press today, especially for growth and expansion of the rural press. While the press in India has been fearlessly exposing defects in public life, it has not paid sufficient attention to the other two objectives of the press namely: *(i)* in understanding popular feeling and giving them expression and *(ii)* arousing among people certain desirable sentiments especially in the context of rural India where majority of India's population lives. In other words, development journalism which is the need of the hour in the context of rural India needs to be given its proper place in the overall development and growth of press in India.

Development journalism does not have to be dull and boring as is the usual perception about it. Development journalism is not just publishing dry statistics strung together. It can be very fascinating story telling of our many-fold achievements which even the worst critics cannot deny that India has made since its independence. But a perceptive journalist can unfold the exciting drama behind the process of achievements and progress made. For example, a human interest story and the drama unfolded in the process of successful implementation of many of the specific programmes/schemes under, say, Jawahar Rozgar Yojana, in a particular village or Taluka could be a fascinating news of interest and relevance to a large number of readers and even others in a rural area.

If the rural life and culture becomes the focus of news coverage, features and other stories of a newspaper, I am sure there will be many subscribers of such a newspaper thereby giving a fillip to circulation of newspapers in rural areas which in turn will attract the advertisers for marketing their goods and services in rural areas. Such a reorientation of press would also facilitate the present national campaign on literacy. It has been observed that many a times many of those who are literate under literacy mission tend to *relapse* into literacy for non-availability of any suitable reading material. Such a movement for Rural Press will supplement and compliment not only our national campaign for universal literacy by the year 2001 but also many other development programmes and campaigns. As a matter of fact, if the press and other mass media reach the rural masses in adequate measure, it will lead to strengthening of democracy and ushering in social and cultural change, thereby facilitating safe transaction into 21st century, not as two distinct entities—'Bharat' and 'India' but as a united and strong India.

This would require, among other things, a large number of trained journalists who are adequately sensitised and oriented to 'shift' their focus from the accepted news values which are urban and western to rural and indigenous. Keeping that in view the Indian Institute of Mass Communication last year decided to open its centres in different regions of the country in relatively smaller places located in rural/tribal milieu.

2

RURAL PRESS
Role in Development

— Anjan Kumar Banerji

It is said, India lives in villages. It is true. India has a population of 800 million, more than half of the population lives in 600,000 villages. Almost half of the population is illiterate. They languish in poverty. They suffer from pestilence and squalor. They are faced with unemployment and under-employment. There are wrinkles of frustration on every face. This is village India.

Let me pay my homage to Gandhiji, on his 125th birth anniversary, by recalling his words from his book, Rebuilding Indian Villages: Indian villages consist of the following problems : Party feelings and quarrels, Jealousy, Illiteracy, Wickedness, Disunion, Carelessness, Lack of manners, Adherence to old meaningless customs and Cruelty. This is village India.

The Father of the Nation also observed, rather dreamt, may be in vain, may be mistakably, "When our villages are fully developed there will be no dearth in them of men with a high degree of skill and artistic talents. There will be village poets, village artists, village architects, linguists and research workers. In short, there will be nothing in life worth having which will not be had in the villages. Today the villages are dung heaps. Tomorrow they will be like tiny gardens of Eden where dwell highly intelligent folk whom no one can deceive or exploit."

Gandhiji's dream of rebuilding Indian villages is still a far cry even after 47 years of independence. In the context of this dismal situation, the journalists have a great role to play to bring about a new climate. Journalism is a social trust. Journalists are social workers. They are the agents of social change. They should not only inform but also interpret and educate. They should give the message of hopes and aspirations to the teeming millions who live under the clouds of frustration in rural areas. They should guide the people to change the quality of life, through better agriculture and environment, better health and family welfare.

Let us examine how the rural press has helped and can help the situation.

It is a common knowledge that like rural people, Rural Press also is poor. The publisher is Editor, Reporter, Clerk, Advertisement Collector—all rolled into one. From about 332 district headquarter towns, rural newspapers are published which are small in size (four to eight pages) and most of them are one-man show. Some of them have a small printing press with Treadle machine and a few cases of type. They do also small job printing to meet expenses. They collect advertisements from local business men, Stationers, Tailors, Hair-cutting Saloons, Laundry, Coaching Centres, etc. It is like a small cottage industry, not equipped with modern technology.

In their struggle for existence, the rural newspapers sometimes do not adhere to the ethics of Journalism, that is, truthfulness and responsibility, objectivity and fairplay. They are rather eager to cater news with *masala* (spices), to suit the tastes and preferences of the readers who are their masters. Development news is far away from their mind. Their main objective is to push sales anyhow, even then many of them are short-lived. Hence, the contents and presentation of such papers have all the appearance of an unprofessional and unskilled job.

Let me say a few words about the place I come from, that is U.P. which has given seven Prime Ministers, yet a backward State, particularly Eastern U.P. The big newspapers like *AJ, Jagaran, Amar Ujala, Swatantra Bharat, Rastriya Sahara* give lip sympathy to the coverage of rural problems. Small newspapers like *Gandiv, Amrit Prabhat, Bharatdoot,* are a bit better in this respect.

Many of my students, failing to get a regular berth in the newspaper world, have tried to start Rural Press themselves. In most cases their efforts proved futile for the lack of support. Disgusted and frustrated, they finally left the press world. Some are still there, but struggling and starving. Recently, one of my lady-students started a Daily newspaper with rural bias from Varanasi. The paper, financed by Gramin Bank, was out with fan-fare. After two months, the lady came to me to announce the death of the newspaper because of rural politics.

The most important aspect of the Rural Press is its contents, that is, message. The rural newspapers should be the mirror of the local people—their worries and anxieties, their troubles and tribulations. Hence, they should deal with development programmes initiated by the Govt. for alleviation of the poverty of the rural people.

They should also work for the implementation of the national slogans—Education for all, Health for All. They should highlight the Integrated Rural Development Programme for the people's participation. They may make efforts to revamp the rural co-operatives, integrated scheme of rural credit and the Primary Land Development Banks Project. They can also participate in Jawahar Rojgar Yojana, Operation Black Board, TRYSEM Scheme, Indira Avas Yojana, and Rural Water Supply particularly Million Wells Scheme and Sanitation programme. Their readers will feel attracted as all these schemes will touch different segments of the rural people. The government also will feel sympathetic and helpful to the rural press, though they should not work as gramophone of the government; they should maintain their independence. Despite enormous expansion of educational facilities in the last 40 years, the literacy rate in India is only 36 per cent. According to the Report of the Committee on Status of Women India (1974), all India rural female literacy was 13.2 per cent. Launched with the slogàn, 'Each One, Teach One', the National Literacy Mission aims at imparting functional literacy to 800 lakh adult illiterates in 15-35 age group by 1995. It is difficult to understand why can't we involve Rural Press with National Literacy Mission which has an allocation of Rs. 14,000 crores under the Eighth Plan.

It is also not understood, why can't we involve Rural Press with the Rural Development Programme which has also an allocation of Rs. 30,000 crores under the Eighth Five Year Plan? Why can't the Govt. grant postal and telephone concessions besides liberal supply of newsprints and government advertisements? The Government Fact-Finding Committee on Newspaper Economics stated, "There is no reason why a small newspaper should not get the type of assistance which is normally available to small industry". Can't the Khadi & Village Industries Commission and Gramin Banks treat the Rural Press as a Village Industry?

It is true that the All India Newspaper Editors Conference (AINEC), Indian Newspaper Society (INS), Indian Federation of Working Journalists (IFWJ) and Press Council of India had no time and mind to think of the Rural Press. But why not the Directorate of Field Publicity of the Ministry of Information & Broadcasting start again the features on success stories on Development? Why not Directorate of Audio-Visual Publicity (DAVP) release again Hamara Desh? Why not multi-media campaign of the Govt. for Economic Reforms is associated with the Rural Press? Why not Publication Division bring out monographs for rural women and rural labour? Why not Press Information Bureau take some interest in the development and welfare of the Rural Press? Why not the University Grants Commission organise a series of workshops and Refresher Courses on Rural Press, as was done in Banaras Hindu University and Gujarat Vidyapeeth last year for the teachers of Indian Universities?

In the midst of the clouds, we find silver lining in the words of Prime Minister Narasimha Rao, "It will be our endeavour to improve the quality of lives for the millions of our people who are living in want and deprivation. The betterment of the rural poor will receive the government's closest attention."

There is also a ray of hope at the advent of a new dawn in the economic life of India, particularly village India because of installation of Panchayati Raj institutions which have a major role to play for the building of a new India. We have come along way since the days of 'Village Chatera', a brain-child of B. G. Verghese, then with the *Hindustan Times.* We have come a long way since the days of Brick by Brick' of Kuldip Nayar in the *Statesman.* We have also come a long way since a series of Workshops for the Rural Journalists by the Press Institute of India under Chanchal Sarkar in Collaboration with the Press Foundation of Asia and also since the days of National Seminar at Agra by the International Press Institute in association with Friedrich Nauman Stiftung or Lesley Sawhney programme at Deolali or since the AMIC Seminar in Bangalore in 1975. Now is the time to think of another Fact-Finding Committee on Newspaper Economics after 20 years. Now is the time to have a Rural Press Commission. Let the Indian Institute of Mass Communication give a new dimension to the Rural Press in its task for Rural Development.

3

RURAL NEWSPAPERS
Case Study of a Project

— *K. S. Ramakrishnan*

The Research Institute for Newspaper Development (RIND), a society promoted by major newspapers in India and having its office in Madras, has been in the forefront in advocating the publication of rural newspapers ever since its inception in 1979.

With financial assistance from Sijthoff Press of Netherlands (100,000 Dutch Guilders) and Cuesot-Loire of France (25,000 US Dollars), RIND has implemented a Kannada Rural Newspaper Project at Sagar in Karnataka State since 1985-86.

Under this project, four prospective editor-proprietors in Sagar and adjacent areas were selected and given training, both in editorial and managerial aspects, of running weekly newspapers which will cover events in their respective areas.

For the composition and printing of the newspapers, RIND set up a central production facility, under the name 'RIND Rural Press', at Sagar. This facility consisted of a Berthold Autologic phototypesetting system, an AB Dick 385 offset printing machine, and the required ancillary equipment, including a Ravenna camera and Agfa Gavaert processor.

When RIND formulated the project in 1985, no software was available for computer composition in Kannada language. RIND, therefore, gave considerable assistance to M/s Autologic of Switzerland to develop the software. The initial proposal of RIND was that each of the editors in the project would be given a stand-alone front-end computer in which he could compose all material needed for his newspaper, save the material in a floppy disc and bring it to Sagar, where the output could be got from the phototypesetting system for further page make–up and printing. M/s Autologic who had initially agreed to develop the complete software for this purpose could do so only for the centralised inputting and phototypesetting system, and could not develop the software for the stand-alone systems. Consequently, the editorial matter for all the four newspapers had to be composed centrally at Sagar itself, necessitating the editors to spend a day or two every week at Sagar where they attended to the proof-reading, guided the page make-up, and collected the printed copies for distribution among their subscribers.

The four weekly newspapers under the project were started between October, 1986 and April, 1987. Each issue consisted of 8 pages of the size 11" x 8", and covered news of a taluk (tehsil). They became quite popular within a short period, and built up circulation figures of 800 to 1200, but with a readership of not less than 5000 each. Each copy was priced at Re. 1, with subscription rates of Rs. 13 for a quarter, Rs. 25 for half-year and Rs. 45 for a year.

Subsequently, in 1987, there was a welcome and cost-effective technological development. The Apple Macintosh Desk Top Publishing System had made its entry into India, and its local agents had developed the software for composition in Kannada language. The main advantage of this system was that a camera-ready output of composed matter could be obtained on plain paper, as against the expensive photographic material that the Autologic phototypesetting system required. Moreover, the Apple Macintosh inputting and editing terminal was basically a stand-alone system, the floppy disc from which could be transported and used for getting the final output from a laser printer at a central place.

RIND, therefore, decided to switch over to this more cost-effective pre-press system, and submitted a project proposal to the Foundation Communication Development Cooperation of Netherlands Government (which was subsequently renamed as Communication Assistance Foundation), which provided for the replacement of the phototypesetter at Sagar with two Apple laser printers, and the procurement of seven Apple Macintosh computers. CAF made a liberal contribution of Rs. 475,000 for this purpose. This enabled RIND to give an Apple Macintosh computer to each editor which he could use at his own premises for initial composition of news stories.

For the first two years, the production cost of the newspapers was fully subsidised by RIND, which paid for the newsprint and other consumables and also met the establishment charges such as rent, staff expenses, etc. in the central facility. The direct subsidy was progressively reduced and was completely withdrawn in 1992, after which RIND undertook to meet only the establishment expenses of the Rural Press. It was planned to withdraw this hidden subsidy also progressively.

Though the newspapers under the project fulfilled a felt need and had gained popularity, there were lapses in the renewal of subscriptions. Though the newspapers themselves enjoyed concessional postage, any correspondence relating to them had to incur normal postage, which had progressively increased from 25 paise to Re. 1 for a simple letter. For a low-value product such as the rural newspaper, with a cover price of only Re. 1, and a quarterly subscription rate of only Rs. 13, it was uneconomic to send more than a couple of reminders to defaulters. Travelling to villages for the renewal campaign was even more expensive. The price of newsprint had also registered an increase of nearly 40 per cent between 1987 and 1991. Increase in the cover-price could become counter-productive, because it could result in a further fall in the circulation figure.

There were not enough business enterprises in the areas covered by these newspapers for them to receive sustenance from advertisements.

The concept on which RIND had implemented the project was that rural newspapers required subsidy only during the initial period, after which they would become sufficiently viable financially, giving a reasonable level of income to the editor/publisher for his labour. But, due to the foregoing reasons, the viability of the publications promoted by it initially had become eroded. RIND itself did not have access to further funds to continue the subsidy to them.

In the meantime, four more residents in the areas nearby Sagar had approached RIND with the request that they may also be assisted by it for publishing similar newspapers. Since spare capacity was available in its Rural Press, RIND agreed to their request on condition that they would not be given any direct subsidy, and they would have to meet the cost of newsprint and printing from the beginning. Because these individuals had other means of income and were not dependent on any profit from the newspapers, they had agreed to this condition. They were also in a position to absorb the incidental expenses relating to the newspapers, such as postage and clerical cost, in their other businesses.

The result was that, while the newspapers which were promoted by RIND had to discontinue publication because the editor/publishers selected by it did not have the financial means to publish them without continued subsidy, the Rural Press Project is still successfully running because four other entrepreneurial individuals are using the facility, and are successfully publishing the papers from there.

From RIND's experience with this project, it could be inferred :

1. There is definitely a role and need for rural newspapers in Indian conditions.

2. The readership of rural newspapers is much larger than their circulation.

3. The Desk Top Publishing technology, together with an inexpensive tabletop offset printing machine, is well-suited for the production of a rural newspaper.

4. The pricing of the paper has an impact on its circulation figure because of the low purchasing power of the prospective subscribers, and the newspaper has to necessarily be a low-priced product.

5. For some more years at least, till rural businesses pick up, it is difficult for rural newspapers to get any substantial advertisement revenue that will offset the production cost.

6. The progressive increase in newsprint prices and postal tariff militate against keeping the rural newspaper a low-priced product, thereby affecting its circulation.

7. With lower circulation, the unit cost of production goes up, contributing to the non-viability of the publication still further.

8. In the present conditions, a rural newspaper cannot become viable enough to meet its own costs and also yield a modest living income to the editor/publisher if he takes it up as his full-time occupation.

9. A rural newspaper is, however, a viable proposition if some of its incidental expenses, such as postage and clerical assistance, are absorbed by some other business belonging to the editor/publisher, and he does not depend upon the newspaper for earning his livelihood.

RIND is quite satisfied that, in spite of difficulties that the project had to face, four rural weekly newspapers are being published on a regular basis from its central facility in Sagar.

4

RURAL PRESS
Its Present and Future

— G. P. Jain

Before we crystal gaze the future of the Rural Press, let us understand the present state of the rural press as also of the people it seeks to serve, because the two interact on each other. If the village people are prosperous, industry would want to go to them to mop up their savings. Industry will then need the rural press to carry its sales message. A self-sufficient or well-to-do rural press will be in a strong position to educate, inform and advise its readers.

It is a sad fact that India is not one country, but two countries. One is, by comparison, developed and the other un-developed or under-developed. One is urban India, the other rural India. True, there are slums in the urban area also, just as there are slums in America and Japan, too. But, by and large, the distinction holds.

Let alone a high level of literacy or economic viability, a quarter of our villages do not even have clean drinking water. Many villages in the interior are still sealed tight against external intrusion, except when their squabbles spill over making it necessary for them to go to a police station or court. Most producers sell their small surplus produce in their village itself.

How will a rural paper function in such an atmosphere and how should it go about establishing a communication link with rural India?

I came to the conclusion in the very beginning that it would not be advisable to harp on agriculture alone, which is the life's grind of the rural people. They get sick of it often, though they have no alternative and have to stick around. A paper, in order to catch their attention, has to satisfy their hunger for news—the more spicy the better—of social as well as political nature. The rural people are relentless gossips. They sit down whenever they can and gab about this or that matter. This provides them the only entertainment possible. They are the most well-informed about their neighbours.

The future of the rural press is as bleak or as rosy as the future of the rural people it serves. When the benefits of planning begin to percolate to the lower levels and the life in rural India improves, the readers will gladly pay for the service they will demand from the rural press. If one were to ask me if there were newspaper readers in the villages, those who want to cull the store information acquired from newspapers, I shall say most certainly there are such readers now.

Let's take Uttar Pradesh. Even as things stand, it is saturated with 875 Development Blocks. Each Block headquarters is manned by a team of 10-15 development officials. Each Block receives 20-30 people everyday. Those among them who can read are our potential readers who without spending their money want to soak up what they can during their short visit to the Block headquarters for communication to their neighbours during impromptu gatherings. Lakhs of potential readers are also available in Cooperative Societies, Krishak Charcha Mandals, Village Panchayats and Schools.

A Beginning Made

An attempt has been made by enterprising men to take the press to the countryside. Farm papers in various Indian languages, with their content and presentation tailored to the needs and grasp of the rural readers, have appeared in different States of India. The rural press shows promise, but it still has a long distance to travel.

Journalism in a developing country like ours does not have to strike a posture of confrontation against the Government. The relationship between the two, especially between Government and the Rural Press, should be one of friendly cooperation. What one, as editor of a rural newspaper, may attempt to do is to make his readers wise about the various development programmes launched by Government for rural development and bring their reactions on implementation to Government officers and political leaders. It, in fact, serves as a link between Government and the people in a more pronounced manner than any other segment of the press. Not to be accused of drum-beating for Government, the communicator should also point out the shortcomings in planning as well as implementation of Government programmes.

Development journalism, which is the need of the hour in the Third World, does not have to be dull and boring. Not dry statistics strung together, but the exciting drama behind the process of achievement could be unfolded interestingly. For example, a story on bank loans to the economically weaker sections of the society which is a recent phenomenon in India could either be packed with statistical progress year by year, or it could unravel the story of how unpriviledged men and women used the loan to start out on new productive careers. Such a story when read in the countryside might ignite a bush fire of wide acceptance. This is what I mean by friendly cooperation.

A rural paper, I can speak from my 28 years' experience as Editor of *Sevagram Weekly* published from Delhi, will have a great and loyal readership, if it can also fight for them. Not a day passes when an injustice is not perpetrated on a village community by the rich few or underlings of bureaucracy. Like a social worker, a rural paper can win the people's confidence and trust if it takes up their causes in a crusading spirit. I can cite several examples. To give you one example, in the tehsil headquarters of Sikandrabad in Bulandshahr district of Uttar Pradesh, revenue mutation proceedings in respect of 350 acres of common village land illegally appropriated by a half dozen rich men were in their last stage when we got scent of it. We raised the matter in our columns, led a delegation of the poor people to the Collector and got the land distributed to them. In the process we picked up many readers and our credibility was enhanced. What the urban press did during the independence struggle for the national cause, the rural press can do now for rural communities.

Adult Literacy

An ambitious adult literacy plan has been launched in the country. A three or six-month crash programme will not be enough for permanent results. The rural press can and should play a major role in the follow-up operations. Three components of the adult literacy drive are promotion of literacy, functional skill and social awareness. The rural press can achieve the third objective splendidly. It can also play a significant role in the post-literacy phase. The neo-literate's hunger for knowledge denied to him until now can well be quenched by addition of suitable reading columns.

The main purpose of the rural press, however, is to carry the message of better farming to its readers. Agricultural demonstrations on the farmers' fields are organized by farm universities and research bodies. The results of these need to be carried for wider acceptance. Unfortunately, Government magazines are not as convincing as the professional press.

The written word enjoys far more credibility than the spoken word and endures longer. Anything printed in a newspaper carries the aura of uncontestability. To the village people, especially, the written word is sacred. Besides, a rural paper need not be a shabby specimen. It should give them the best in presentation. SEVAGRAM got the second National Award in printing and designing in 1975 among all the Indian language publications.

If, despite TV and radio, the urban press is expected to generate newer demand for consumer articles, the rural press can also be expected to do a similar job in the countryside both for production inputs and consumption articles. Even today, with vigorous selling many more village people can be persuaded to buy such new articles which would bring them physical comfort or credit for being consumer pioneers. The opportunity is still limited, because according to Government statistics, 50 per cent of farm households in the country do not own more than one hectare of agricultural land (33 per cent own less than 1/2 hectare). Those owning more than 4 hectares are only 15 per cent of the total population. But with the growth of agriculture and industry, the sale of consumer articles is bound to grow. The rural press can accelerate the process.

Catching the Readers

The most vexing question is how to get the rural people read the Rural Press. There are no news agents or hawkers in the villages. In many places, there is no railhead. Selling subscription for a potential agent is not remunerative. The readers are anxious to read, but they cannot spare the money. Several times at such seminars the question of Government subsidy to the rural press has cropped up. I have always held the view that subsidy is not what is needed. It's the subscriptions that will give the rural paper standing with the advertisers who will foot the high cost of production and distribution. The solution thus is that the Government should buy subscriptions to good papers and ask them to supply direct to the panchayat leaders, school teachers and other opinion-makers in the villages. A prestigious magazine like *Reader's Digest* still launches a drive for complimentary subscriptions. The rural press needs them most. But I very much doubt if this suggestion will be accepted, because each Government department is interested to bring out its own departmental journal on glossy paper with the departmental head as its chief editor. You can well visualize what it would achieve.

I say very strongly that one of the major reasons for the failure of most Government plans is the absence of a strong rural press to educate, inform and advise its readers week after week or month after month (a rural daily is still a thing of distant future).

Much is said from public platforms about the need for a vibrant rural press. Even the urban press is exhorted to go to villages, but the irony is that those rural papers which are already in existence are languishing for want of official encouragement. Little said the better about private industry.

Unhelpful Official Attitude

The Rural Press is not only ignored but also scorned by the urban elite as well as the Government. It's not surprising, because it cannot enjoy greater merit than what its readers (the village people) get from society or the Government. Even such Government spokesmen whose duty it is to keep themselves well-informed about the press give hardly a minute of their time to what is written in the rural press. I doubt if an editorial from any rural paper is put up before any Minister or policy-maker. By rural paper, I do not mean the politically-oriented mofussil press. A rural paper is one, as defined by the Indian Rural Press Association, which devotes at least 40 per cent of its editorial space to agriculture, horticulture, community development, cooperatives and panchayati raj, etc.

Viewing the future of the rural press in the perspective I have presented to you, I feel that the rural press has many more years of persistent struggle ahead before it is recognized as a significant segment of the Indian Press. Today, it is the weaker section of the Indian Press. The future of the rural press is no better or more assured than the future of the rural people it serves. If 45 per cent of our people continue to live below the poverty line, the immediate future of the rural press is not very bright.

5

RURAL PRESS DEVELOPMENT
Problems and Perspectives

— *V. S. Gupta*

India is predominantly a rural country—a land of villages. Notwithstanding the rapid industrial and technological progress made by India since independence, the Indian economy is basically agricultural. A little over one-third of the country's national income is derived from agriculture and allied activities, which absorbs about two-thirds of its working force.

The cultural ethos and milieu of India is rural. The Indian fairs and festivals are organised to celebrate the bountiful gift of nature—coinciding with the two crop cycles — *rabi* and *kharif.* An average Indian farmer is a hard working, honest and sincere person deeply attached to his farm, fields and livestock. The rural areas are repositories of rich cultural heritage. The Indian tradition of dance and music has strong rural roots. Not only this, the objectives of planned economic development since 1952, the beginning of the planning era—has been to ensure that rural areas are provided with viable means of economic growth.

All this should have made the rural areas of India bustling with prosperity. The rural scenario, however, is not that optimistic. A large majority of villages do not get a newspaper or a magazine. There are virtually no retail outlets for books, magazines or newspapers in rural areas. The library system, which, in any case, is poor even in towns, does not exist in villages. As such the rural reading habit does not exist. No wonder, exposure of villages to literacy and consequently to the press has been so poor. The dismal situation exists in spite of the massive efforts undertaken by the government to ameliorate the conditions of rural poverty ever since the beginning of planned economic development since early fifties.

Rural development, in the broad sense of the term, holds the key to all economic progress, industrial or agrarian, urban or rural.

For conveying the message of development to the rural population, as also keeping the administrators, planners and policy-makers posted with reactions and aspirations, rural press constitutes an enduring and viable instrument, as a part of effective media strategy.

Rural Press

The rural press, as a medium for community communication, with its potential for creating awareness of, and articulating, people's problems; as a link between the policy-makers, development bureaucracy and farmers; as a second line of conversion of scientific knowledge into information for utilization in the field situation, imparting adult education and also as a vehicle for reinforcing the literacy habit, is being increasingly recognised as an important and viable means for the promotion of social awareness and national development.

It is a promising medium for disseminating information and knowledge about nutrition, health and hygiene, improved farm practices, family planning measures and development plans to those sections of the society where the information is needed most. Special attention has been paid to its problems, prospects and promotion by several organizations such as, UNESCO (which had launched a project for encouraging the Rural Press in Africa in the early seventies), the International Programme for Development Communication (IPDC), and other United Nations agencies under the programme of Development Support Communication (DSC). The growing interest in the rural press by these organizations and now even by newspapers published from metropolitan centres, augurs well and testifies to the important role that the rural press can play as an integral part of the rural communication development process.

The Indian Rural Press Association (IRPA) defines a rural paper as one which devotes at least 40 per cent of its editorial space to agriculture, horticulture, community development, cooperation and Panchayati Raj, etc. "A rural paper would essentially be a language paper published from outside the metropolitan and big cities and most probably from a district headquarters. It is essentially a small newspaper, which as per the classification of the Registrar of the Newspapers of India (RNI) will primarily have a circulation below 15,000 copies. It caters to local issues of immediate importance to the people". According to another definition, a rural newspaper is one that, "is primarily published from a rural area, devoting at least 50 per cent of its contents to the problems relating to the rural community, in a language akin to the idion of the rural readers."

The community newspapers by definition are the papers, "located outside the capital and their focus is more on local news."

The regional press with its grassroots contacts through a network of correspondents in district towns, touching upon local issues and topical subjects relevant to the common man, concerning his everyday life and written in a style close to his head and heart, enjoys a large measure of similarity with the rural press as far as language, local interest and subject spread is concerned. Some regional newspapers brought out from bigger towns have large circulations and multi editions.

The Rural Press, therefore, shares most of the characteristics of the community newspapers, local newspapers and the regional press. Several experts on the subject have, therefore, been using these terms interchangeably, notwithstanding certain differences in their circulation, subject spread, etc. Some of the regional papers, may, for instance, have a larger circulation and cover a vast range of topics from sports to national politics, etc. In such cases it could perhaps be too far fetched to classify these papers as the rural press. The following statement may, therefore, generally be the most acceptable concept of the rural press.

When we refer to the rural press we mean small newspapers with small circulation, serving small communities and catering to their special needs and interests, that cannot be met by the urban press.

Role of Rural Press

Wilbur Schramm, in his book, *Mass Media and National Development,* considered rural newspapers as one of the great movers of national development. Such a newspaper gives the neo-literate reason to learn to read better and makes public participation in governmental policies more informed, relevant and meaningful. Apart from broadening the actual educational base of its readers, the rural papers break down the barriers of isolation and provide written material to the villagers who have learnt to read so that they can apply their reading ability to increase their production.

Reinforcing Literacy

The printed word, particularly in the rural areas, has a fascination of its own. It is a catalyst of change and growth. To improve the recognition, understanding and appreciation of the printed word, specially for those for whom it is not a routine matter to interact with books and newspapers, is a worthwhile task. Aldous Huxley has said, "Every man who knows how to read has to magnify himself, to multiply the way in which he exists, to make his life full, significant and interesting." The rural newspaper, with its simple language and contents closest to the interest of its readers, reinforces this reading habit, day in and day out. Since reading is basic to the understanding of the working of a host of social, economic and political institutions, the rural press, by cultivating and reinforcing the reading habit, performs an important role in the process of social and political awareness.

The International Commission for the Study of Communication Problems, while summarising its recommendations, says : The development of a community press in rural areas and small towns would not only provide print support for economic and social extension activities. This would also facilitate the production of functional literature for neo-literates as well.

In a seminar on Publishing for Rural Areas in Developing Countries, the well known thinker, Dr. Rajni Kothari was quoted as under : "Acquisition of a minimum education level greatly raises a person's skill and his capacity to enter the employment market; it also raises his sense of potency and his ability to relate himself to the outside world, his sense of political efficacy, and his general self-confidence and sense of dignity."

If the rural press were to serve its function of "reinforcing literacy" or preventing readers from lapsing into illiteracy once again, it would have fulfilled a task of great national importance, and particularly so in developing countries where illiteracy continues to be a serious problem.

Emphasising the need and importance of rural press, in the famous treatise, *Communication and Change in the Developing Countries,* one of the pioneering efforts focusing on the above subject; Nair has stated:

> Some times it has been asked whether the host of small district newspaper which have come out in recent years serve any useful purpose. They are said to confine their attention mainly to local complaints and disputes. I have regarded these district papers as of immense value, for, they focus the attention of the local population on local development effort and assist in creating interest in the local affairs. I personally know of a number of cases in which these small. newspapers have exercised considerable influence on local administration and have helped to build local opinion on political and economic issues. If development requires local participation, these district papers have to play an important role in mobilizing

local effort. It may be conceded that all of them are not motivated by the highest ideals, and some of them may be instruments of local politicians, but as a whole they are of great assistance to local development. Political decentralization and establishment of Panchayati Raj have created a new political structure in local administration. The Zila Parishads and Panchayat Samitis have been entrusted with wide powers in the spheres of local administration and local development. The small district newspapers have the same significance in local affairs as provincial papers in state matters and metropolitan papers in national problems. The study team on Five Year Plans publicity has described this section of the press as the most important link in the communication chain. There can be little doubt of what a healthy mofussil press can do to inculcate high ideals of public service and a sense of dedication to people's weal and welfare in the making of the local self-governing institutions.

According to Yadava: "If the rural life and culture becomes the focus of news coverage, features and other stories of a newspaper, I am sure there will be many subscribers of such a newspaper thereby giving a fillip to circulation of newspapers in rural areas which in turn will attract the advertisers for marketing their goods and services in rural areas. Such a reorientation of press would also facilitate the present national campaign on literacy. It has been observed that many a times many of those who are literate under literacy mission tend to relapse into literacy for non-availability of any suitable reading material. Such a movement for rural press will supplement and complement not only our national campaign for universal literacy by the year 2001 but also many other development programmes and campaigns. As a matter of fact if the press and other mass media reaches rural masses in adequate measure, it will lead to strengthening of democracy and ushering in social and cultural change, thereby facilitating safe transaction into 21st century, not as two distinct entities — 'Bharat' and 'India' but as a united and strong India."

Second Level of Conversion

A rural newspaper provides a forum to articulate the urges of the common man. It takes up local issues and immediate requirements, affecting the people. It gives greater importance to the problems agitating the ordinary people; unemployment, scarcity of agricultural inputs, the law and order situation at the village level, etc. It is best suited to act as the second level of conversion of scientific knowledge into information in a usable form for the benefit of the ultimate clientele—the farmers.

It is well recognised that, by and large, the first conversion of scientific knowledge into information takes place at the level of research institutions. Literature produced at this stage for common consumption can be utilized by the educated and high level functionaries having access to such literature. Such information is further converted, for the second time, in the form of newspapers, pamphlets, newsletters and magazines, and transferred through the government extension agencies to the lower level government functionaries like the Village Level Workers (VLWs) or the Agricultural Development Officers (ADOs). It is here that the Rural Press plays perhaps its most important role. This role is, in fact, the primary role that most of the rural extension papers and magazines brought out by the agricultural universities and state departments of agriculture, are performing. In the absence of the rural press, the knowledge generated in the experimental fields and laboratories of research institutions and universities would have remained confined to the files of the researchers and scientists.

Source of Development Information

It is not only with respect to the scientific knowledge that the rural press works as the second level of conversion. It also plays an important role as conveyer of information about development plans and programmes of the government, such as availability of seeds and fertilizers and loans through the banks, and the cooperative societies, market rates of agricultural produce, etc. It establishes a link between government functionaries and the village and fills the much needed gap in the information process. It has been widely accepted that so long as the rural population does not possess information processing capacity to use opportunities made available by the government, the massive economic inputs notwithstanding, the fruits of planned development will not reach the poor, those living below the poverty line and whose economic status the government plans profess to improve. The rural press is remarkably suited to fill in this missing link between the development functionaries and the users and consumers of development information.

The rural press is also expected to, and in many cases does, perform the role of a crusader on behalf of its readers. The well known rural journalist, G. P. Jain, has written about the rural press, in *Seminar,* in its issue on *The Village and the Communicator* :

A rural paper, I can speak from my 25 years experience, will have a great and loyal readership, if it can also fight for its readers. Not a day passes without an injustice being perpetrated on a village community by the rich few or the underlings of bureaucracy. Like a social worker, a rural paper can win the people's confidence and trust if it takes up their causes in a crusading spirit. What the urban press did during the independence struggle for the national cause, the rural press can do now for the rural communities and earn their great gratitude.

A similar role for the rural press—that of reporting injustice being done to the people living in villages under the tyranny of the rich and the powerful—was pointed out by another eminent journalist, D. R. Mankekar, who said that crime unreported was crime licensed and encouraged and, therefore, it would be the duty of the papers working in rural areas to expose such injustice to the people.

According to a UNESCO study on rural newspapers in Africa, the rural press ensure's a dialogue between "rural environment and urban environment".

A significant feature of the rural press is its closer identity with the people on account of emotional and linguistic affinity. The English language newspapers are more analytical in their approach and are interested in broader subjects like functioning of international institutions, legislative reforms, separation of the judiciary from the executive, economic reforms, etc. They do not articulate the urges of the common man; whereas the editors of rural or district newspapers give greater importance to the problems concerning the common man—unemployment, rising prices, law and order difficulties at the local level, etc. The rural newspapers which are in contact with the grassroot levels, and are aware of the local problems, will be able to communicate in the language and idiom that the people understand.

The rural newspaper is in touch with the day-to-day life problems of the common man : a small scale or marginal farmer, rural artisan, village school teacher. The literature and information produced by the rural press—profile of an artisan, success story of a progressive farmer, problems faced in the marketing of agricultural produce, social superstitions and taboos inhibiting economic growth and productivity—not only reflect the life in the villages, but also provide a different perspective and frame of reference for planners and policy-makers. The feedback so available would be of great help for reorienting development plans. Like the local radio stations, the rural press also serves as the source of information about various schemes, plans, projects and facilities available like credit, seed, fertilizer.

Scope of Rural Press

The rural press evolves its own editorial and news structure as also its own vocabulary. As to the resource personnel, it generally has school teachers, community development workers, agricultural extension workers and the local legislator as writers and contributors. Written in the simple, regional language of the area, the press is ideally suited to be a People's Forum through which people's grievances may be conveyed to the authorities in the district. It will, thus, encourage a two way flow of information, rather than being unidirectional which most of the mass media is at present.

Rural newspapers are the most suitable medium for localised programming. Through locally produced news and commentaries, feature articles, interviews, pictures, stories and letters to the editor, the newspaper can stir up interest, initiate discussion and serve as a sounding board for audience reaction.

According to the research findings on Agricultural Journalism and Rural Development, the *Research Bulletin No. 35* brought out by the Division of Agricultural Extension, Indian Agricultural Research Institute: The question of effectiveness of content is linked with the background of writers who contribute articles in farm periodicals. On the whole, readers have attached more authenticity to scientists and extension workers. However, readers regarded the articles written by them to be too scientific and technical in nature. Thus, there is a need to have scientists and extension workers as writers who could write without the theoretical bias and have a first hand knowledge of field problems. They will have to acquire techniques of writing technical articles in simple language by using local equivalents for technical terms. To gear the scientists to the task of writing for farmers is a difficult proposition, mainly because of their bias and preference for research paper writing. To improve the situation, it is necessary that scientists be given certain incentives and some short term training in writing for farmers. The short term training courses can be organised by agricultural universities and extension departments. This would help them in writing articles in a simple language.

Regarding the ideal content-mix, G. P. Jain has some very interesting observations to make :

> I came to the conclusion in the very beginning that it would not be advisable to harp on agriculture alone, which is a grind. Villagers get sick of it although they have no alternative profession and have

to stick around. A paper, in order to catch their attention, has to satisfy their hunger for news—the more spicy, the better—of a social as well as political nature. Rural people are relentless gossips. They sit down when they can and crap about this or that matter. This provides them their only entertainment. They are also most well informed about the neighbours.

The rural press, by and large, apart from giving news also gives expression to the concerns of its readers, more than the metropolitan press does, as it is situated closer to the homes and hearth of its readers.

Constraints

One of the most formidable obstacles that a rural newspaper has to overcome is limited sales and circulation which creates a discouraging situation : since the circulation is limited, advertisements will not be readily forthcoming and without advertisements, the paper will find it hard to survive—a dismal situation indeed for any rural paper.

One of the most effective methods, tried successfully by the author who headed the Farm Information Communication Service (FICS) during 1973-76, in promoting the sales of its farm monthly magazine, *Haryana Kheti,* was through launching a sales and subscription campaign. The method used was simple. All the subscribers on the mailing list of the magazine were requested to enrol one more member for the publication. They were requested to pass on our circular letter to their neighbours, friends and the Panchayat Samitis. They were also requested to convey the request by word of mouth. The response was beyond expectations, indeed it was heart warming. Some of the members who had been loyal readers for years wrote back to us after complying with one request. Some others wrote personal letters saying that they had not only conveyed the message of enrolling more subscribers for the magazine, but also ensured that money orders had actually been sent. Others wrote that they were not getting the magazine regularly.

We were surprised to note that for some of the subscribers, the magazine was the only window to the university which again was the only institution they had known except for the traditional village institutions like the Panchayats or the village school. The campaign gave us an opportunity not only to increase the sales and subscription of our magazine, but also provided us with excellent feedback from the readers.

During recent years, a large number of organizations dealing with rural interests—agricultural universities, research institutions, agricultural input agencies, cooperative societies and marketing federations—have taken up extension work in the villages. They organize farmers' fairs, field days on demonstration plots, workshops for releasing recommendations on different crops. These occasions provide a valuable opportunity to the publishers of the rural papers and their readers to interact with each other.

Advertising Support for Rural Press

Advertising, which has been confined largely to the urban areas, is now gaining a foothold in rural areas. The reasons are many : massive investment of government funds in the field of rural development resulting in more money in the hands of rural consumers, extension of the electronic media in villages at a rapid pace, and the consistent efforts of commercial enterprises and big business houses to enter the rural market. With planned economic development measures initiated by the government, the village people are emerging as major consumers. Also, the advent of high yielding varieties which has contributed to the economic prosperity and agricultural boom has increased the demand for consumer goods. Several other measures, almost everywhere in the Asian villages—electrification, rural banking, postal and telecommunication facilities and greater interaction with urban areas—are directing the villages towards a market economy. All this, in turn, had led to a boom in rural advertising.

The complaint of the small and rural newspapers in the Indian situation is : whereas in terms of circulation the English language newspapers are far behind the language papers, more than half of the budgetary provision of the central government for advertisement is allocated to the former. More distressing is the fact that advertisements aimed at creating social awareness, directed primarily at the rural masses, are released to the urban newspapers.

In this context, local advertising is the one area which the rural press should sincerely and vigorously strive to capture. With the increasing prosperity and economic activity in rural communities in all countries of Asia, improved transport and communication systems, and accelerated demand for consumer goods, local advertising by the local branches, offices and other commercial advertisements originating from small scale industry will be substantial. Then there are a large number of institutions operating from district headquarters : municipal committees, district courts, banks, etc. They constitute a potential source of advertisements. Additionally, there would be scope for tapping social community advertisements, like notices of births, marriages, obituary notices, political and social meetings, election meetings, etc. in ample measure, which would constitute a rich source of advertisement support.

The participants from various Asian countries at the seminar on the Development of Rural Press in Asia, organised by the AMIC in November 1986, were of the opinion that potential existed both for readership and advertisement support for the community and rural press in the region. In the above seminar, the Director, Research Institute for Newspaper Development, C. G. K. Reddy, made the following observations which, by and large, sum up the local advertising situation:

> The need exists for small and rural newspapers, but the rural press must design an appropriate editorial formula that is attractive to the readership in the community. Management must identify the readership and organise itself to reach it. It must also seek the revenue potential and cultivate and exploit the sources fully. Just as readership exists which cannot be served by the urban press, so does advertising potential which cannot be satisfied by the bigger newspapers. The small and rural newspapers must convince themselves that a special clientele exists for them and is waiting to be satisfied. The experience of successful provincial newspapers confirms the view that both readership and advertising potential exist, and this can be exploited to their benefit if newspapers prove they can provide something special and distinct from what the big newspapers are able to.

High Water Mark of Rural Press

The rural press, notwithstanding numerous bottlenecks and problems, has several success stories and shining examples to its credit which could truly be considered as the high water mark of the rural press.

In China, the *Peasants Daily*, the biggest national agricultural four page newspaper has a circulation of one million. It began publication as a weekly in 1980 with a circulation of 200,000. Each copy costs about 60 paise, a price most rural families can afford. It sells in all China's provinces including Tibet, as well as ten foreign countries.

It is indeed remarkable to find that, as a rule, every reporter and editor must spend at least two months in the countryside every year during which time they are expected to familiarize themselves with the local peasants, their aspirations and difficulties.

The paper engages 300 peasants as regular stringers and about 700 as irregular correspondents. The paper chooses the most typical letters for publication while referring the rest to relevant organizations. Very often, investigation groups are sent to the countryside if the letters touch upon matters of significance.

In India, apart from rural newspapers and magazines, agriculture reporting in the big dailies from metropolitan cities has done a lot in creating and sustaining interest on rural topics.

Several universities, cooperative societies and even individuals have been pioneering work in promoting the rural press. They have used this medium for conveying the message of improved agricultural technology to the farmers, livestock keepers, home makers, etc.

The rural press is potentially one of the most effective media for making significant contribution to the economic and social development in the vast rural areas of Asia. This medium will, however, have to the developed into an effective channel of communication. Only then will rural newspapers become instrumental in bringing village communities closer and guide and influence decisions at the level of village institutions.

The doyen of Indian journalists, the late M. Chalapathi Rao, has written, "The future of the Indian press means essentially the future of the Indian language press. India will have gradually mammoth circulation in all the Indian languages". There is no doubt that with increase in literacy and in the purchasing power of the people living in slums in the cities, and in the rural areas, there will be significant increase in the circulation of regional language newspapers, not only in India, but in Asia as a whole.

In a futuristic study on the development of the press in the year 2000, it has been stated that the present public policy against the growth of a monopoly press and in favour of small and medium sized newspapers is likely to continue. The vast size of the country, multiplicity of languages and cultures, and the varying types of regional and local problems also favour the growth of the small and medium sized regional press. With regional development and growth of democratic institutions, a number of newspapers, primarily for the consumption of the literate masses in the rural areas, may also be published. Small and medium sized local newspapers will predominate in the country, but despite their predominance, the big papers published from metropolitan and large cities will share a greater proportion of the total newspaper circulation.

The above discussion underlines the view that rural press has a rich potential, and an educational and constructive role to play in the sphere of nation building. All that is needed is a concerted effort by the media professionals in this direction.

6

MANAGEMENT OF RURAL NEWSPAPERS

—Adarsh Kumar Varma

The most prominent characteristic of a rural newspaper is likely to be that the editorial, business and production functions merge into one. One, two or a handful of persons perform all these functions. The proprietor may also be the editor as well as advertisement and circulation executive in association with a few others—may be a son or sons and/or a brother or brothers. One or more of them may also be composing the matter, making up pages and printing copies of the newspaper.

Perhaps the biggest quality the man running a rural newspaper needs is that he should be a good mixer with leadership qualities and extensive fraternal ties with a cross-section of the people. No ivory tower for him.

This is because much of the work for a rural newspaper has to be honorary. The gain of the person working for a rural newspaper cannot be only, or mainly, financial. Nor would the persons who bring the news or distribute the paper aspire to migrate to a bigger paper which gives greater financial compensation. Anyone working for such a paper does so as a community service which gives him status and prestige in society. He is most likely to be a whole-time peasant or carpenter or shopkeeper and only a part-time worker for the newspaper.

Community Service

This is one of the factors which dictate that the rural newspaper should aim at community service. Health care, sanitation, hygiene, family welfare, improving crop yields, hybrid seeds, irrigation, literacy, education—these and other such subjects have to be the staple which rural newspapers should offer.

The other side of the coin is that the rural newspaper must not even dream of treading the path city-based newspapers take. To take that path will amount to taking on city newspapers on their home ground. Which rural newspaper can thrive on the kind of intensely political reporting and comment which city-based papers like *Jansatta* or *Navbharat Times* carry? If any reader in the catchment area of a rural newspaper is interested in such news and comment, he would rather buy one of these city-based papers than a rural newspaper which tries to imitate them.

Most city newspapers love to report or speculate on inter-party and intra-party squabbling. Urban readers, who are politically oriented because politics is their favourite pastime, gobble it all up. A characteristic of rural areas is that almost no one except for a handful of officials has fixed hours of work, a fixed weekly off, or even a fixed job.

Rural Scene

Village people survive on what they produce. The peasant must till, sow, irrigate and weed his yield. The carpenter must almost everyday find work to do. The man who plies an *ekka* (hackney carriage) must several times a day find people who will hire his vehicle if he is to feed himself, his family and his horse. Good news for him is that one more train will stop at the nearby station everyday, giving him more custom. A new kind of fertilizer which increases the yield by 50 per cent is the best news for the farmer. He would certainly like to know what Pakistan is doing in Kashmir, but the intense diplomatic battles fought by India and Pakistan in Geneva and New York are too distant for him. When, however, such a battle produces a result—say a UN resolution on Kashmir—he would like to know the gist of it. He would also like to know the result of a Test match which India is playing. But the column after column of ball by ball reporting and Sunil Gavaskar's comments cannot be of interest to rural readers.

Rural newspapers can be one of the most powerful media to spread the message of development, hygiene, health, literacy, education, etc. They have a built-in advantage in this area. *Jansatta, Navbharat Times,* the *Hindustan Times* or the *Times of India* just cannot compete with a rural newspaper which is area-specific.

However, there are some built-in disadvantages too. Modern composing and printing machinery are efficient, yielding much more of production than old machinery. They are costly also and need maticulous maintenance. Some need air-conditioning. They are cost-effective when production has to be on a large scale—say several editions of a daily or several newspapers and/or magazines.

This is possible only in cities with their large populations and good train, air and bus connections. Rural newspapers can have a catchment area consisting only of thousands of people, not lakhs. Though mini-machines—like the mini-offset—are being invented, the latest composing and printing machinery are unlikely to be cost effective for rural newspapers.

This is apart from the problem of raising sufficient capital. Even if a man, or a group of men, can raise sufficient capital, they are likely to hesitate to sink it into a rural newspaper. Indeed, hardly anyone is likely to start a rural newspaper for profit. It can only be for communication and community service.

The relatively limited scope for circulation of a rural newspaper means limited scope for obtaining advertisements. Big companies making, for instance, fertilizer are likely to prefer to advertise in town or city-based newspapers with a rural reach rather than in a purely rural newspaper. As for shops selling groceries, cloth or sweets, they are too well known in villages to need advertising. Besides, the small population of villages and relatively low purchasing power mean that there are not many shops and virtually no competition. Where is the need for advertising then?

Special Skills

Yet anyone producing a newspaper, rural or urban, would like his costs to be covered. If that does not happen, even a person with missionery zeal cannot go on producing his paper for any length of time. That is why managing a rural newspaper requires skills which do not have much use in urban newspapers.

As said earlier, the man producing a rural newspaper should have leadership qualities and fraternal ties with a cross-section of society. News gathering in the rural context can be very different from what it is in the urban context. The village *chaupal* where people congregate in the evening can be an effective news exchange. Weddings, illnesses, epidemics, clashes, experience with new fertilizers, etc. are all discussed at these sittings. I am sure the current outbreak of pneumonic plague must be a frequent topic of discussion in many a village *chaupal.* Also many village elders must be coming up with preventive or curative remedies to the disease, some genuine and some imagined, based on experience or hearsay or both, at the *chaupal.*

When someone dies, everyone comes to know of it. Whose son is going to marry whose daughter in which village is also known almost universally. When a boy or girl of the village (or a neighbouring village) graduates or gets a job, it creates a sensation in the rural community. This is in contrast with cities where one may not know where the boy next door works. The major source of non-local news for rural newspapers are the slow-speed news bulletins of All India Radio. They are broadcast for small newspapers and give priority to their needs.

In the rural context, organizing circulation and news gathering have largely to be in the same hands. This is shunned in city-based newspapers because it is supposed to inject an element of commercialism in the editorial section. In rural newspapers this cannot be helped. In any case, there is likely to be very limited of the element of commercialism in rural newspapers. As we have seen, advertising is likely to be very little in rural newspapers. As for circulation, it cannot be based on paid hawkers for the simple reason that no hawker is likely to make enough money to make it worth his while.

The best way to sell copies of the rural newspaper is to put bundles of them at the village grocer's or cloth merchant's or vegetable seller's shop. For a very small commission, or sometimes for no financial consideration but only because it would bring customers to his shop, most grocers or cloth shopkeepers or barbers would gladly sell the newspaper.

It is important to spread out the circulation of rural newspapers to a cluster of villages and to the neighboured railway or bus station. They weekly *hat* or bazar where large numbers of people from several villages come to buy and sell is an important place where the paper's circulation can be pushed.

It is vital to realise in this context that though quantity (or numbers) has its importance, it is not all. Quality or reach to the decision-maker is equally, sometimes even more, important. All of us know that the *Hindustan Times* with its two editions (Delhi and Patna) or the *Statesman* (Calcutta and Delhi) enjoys greater clout and attention at the national level than the *Malayala Manorama* or the *Ananda Bazar Patrika,* which have much larger circulation figures.

It depends on the quality or content of the readership. Who reads the *Malayala Manorama?* Malayalis only, and only those of them who prefer to get their news in their mother tongue. There must be tens of thousands of more Malayalis who read *Malayala Manorama* but also a number of English language papers from Delhi, Calcutta, Bombay or Madras. Besides, I know many Malayalis who get their daily news from English language papers and only occasionally look at Malayalam dailies or periodicals. In Orissa, the *Samaj* published from Cuttack, commands the largest circulation.

Rural newspapers can learn a lesson from this. A rural newspaper widely read in the tehsil town, including 50 villages, may have a circulation of only 20,000. Yet, it is read by the elite of that community.

Can those who wish to convey their message to that rural community, including those who wish to advertise in that area for their products, ignore it?

It is normal for many people to move from their village to one of the neighbouring villages on business. There is usually a primary school in the relatively bigger village or township serving a cluster of villages. The school master or other staff frequently live in another village and commute by bicycle to the school. People who earn their living by driving an *ekka,* a cycle-rickshaw or a push cart usually serve many villages. Bullock-carts are plying all the time from village to village. For more distant villages or townships there is frequently a bus service consisting of one, two or more vehicles. The conductors or drivers of these buses can usually be used by small newspapers in townships and villages to carry bundles of their issues from place to place. All that one has to ensure is that someone is deputed to be at the spot when the bus passes to put bundles of the newspaper in it, with each bundle earmarked and labelled for a particular village. It is also necessary to ensure that the grocer or other shopkeeper who is to sell the copies is always there on time to take delivery of the bundle for his village.

Key Factors

Two key factors have to be stressed in running a rural newspaper. First, a rural newspaper has to be a community newspaper. It must concentrate on giving news of members of the community, and news of interest to them. This kind of news from rural areas is normally out of the reach of city-based newspapers. Yet it is of immense interest to all members of the community. Even the illiterates would like such news to be read out to them. In fact in many cases it is likely to impel them to become literate.

The second key factor is to make the community which the rural newspaper serves as large as possible. A village may consist of a dozen households. Even a big village is unlikely to have more than 500 households, of whom the majority may be illiterate or too poor to afford a newspaper. A rural newspaper is likely to be successful only if it serves a score or more of villages. One reason is that almost everyone knows by word of mouth of what is happening in his village. Printing it does not make it news for him. But most people would learn of something happening in a village 10 km away after several days. The newspaper can speed up the process and the printed word lends authenticity and credibility to the news.

An effort should be made to link the paper to the nearest tehsil or district town. This is because, for most villagers, the nearest town is the promised land. Delhi, Bombay, Calcutta and Madras are for the more adventurous of the villagers or for those already living in district or tehsil towns. What happens in the nearby town is news for villagers. Similarly, town people have no source other than hearsay to get to know what is happening in nearby villages. A rural newspaper can be that source.

Indeed towns without a newspaper of their own have a great disadvantage. The newspapers published from big cities think news from small towns is no news at all unless it is a big fire, an epidemic, starvation, flooding, etc. So, people in towns without a newspaper frequently do not come to know of much of what is happening in the next *mohalla.* A rural newspaper published from a township or big village can fulfil the need.

Managing the news gathering has to be dealt with in some detail. Many outside the newspaper industry do not know that the majority of reporters working for even city-based newspapers are part-time correspondents. They are called stringers. Only a handful of correspondents are paid a regular salary. The bigger newspapers may have a dozen to a score of full-time correspondents plus about half a dozen stringers at the place of publication. They may also have a few staff or special correspondents in the nearest of the state capitals plus a dozen or so stringers in each capital. As for newspapers which are not so big, it is common to manage with three to 10 reporters on the staff and a dozen or so stringers. It is common for the smaller papers, specially if published outside the metropolitan cities, to manage with only one or two staff reporters plus a network of stringers.

The key, once again, is to make the rural newspaper a community media organ. The proprietor most likely will make a meagre living rather than a profit. This is to be expected. Members of the community should be motivated to pitch in with their small contributions by way of voluntary work and, wherever possible, money. Some people who move to various villages in the catchment area may bring in the news from honorary correspondents. Others may be motivated to load 40 or 50 copies of the day's paper on their bicycle and take them to village 10 km away to be put at the village grocer's (or tailor's) shop. He can also bring the sale proceeds of the previous day's edition.

It might not be possible to work all night and distribute the paper next morning. It is likely that different villages would get the paper at different times depending on the time at which the courier of the paper arrives in the village.

To Sum Up

1. The rural newspaper is, and should be, a community service, giving news of immediate interest to the particular rural community. Such news is hot news for members of the community but is usually considered non-news by city-based papers. For non-community news, radio slow-speed and other bulletins are a good source.

2. The news gathering and distribution have largely to be honorary. A hawker system is unlikely to be successful. A better, if unorthodox, distribution system would be to put copies of the paper at the village grocery or other place where people routinely and frequently go.

3. The honorary news gathering system has a proven track record even in city-based journalism. Much of the time first news of an event or happening is broken by stringers, who are part-time correspondents and work not for the money but for the prestige, clout and satisfaction.

4. Financing has to be unorthodox and based on community service and community feeling. Advertisements will be sparse to begin with. The strategy is to go on expanding the catchment area for news gathering and circulation and to include the nearby town, railway station, weekly *hat*, etc. If this can be done, advertisers will find it difficult to ignore rural newspapers.

7

TRAINING OF JOURNALISTS FOR RURAL PRESS

— B. P. Sanjay

The emphasis with regard to communication in India is lopsided in favour of television. Therefore, it was a bit surprising to learn that the organisers of this seminar have identified Rural Press as a focal theme. Their reasons apart, it is imperative that we recognise the importance of the print medium in our communications environment. Many factors—political, economical and technological have sustained this medium. This is also a medium where the direct control of the state is minimum notwithstanding a few attempts to coerce the press through punitive and other measures. Press is also a medium where the sensitive question of ownership and its impact on contents is manifest in various quarters. The current debates on the entry of foreign newspapers through collaborative arrangements is a case in point. Improved telecommunications and the convergence of Information and Communication Technologies (ICTs) have made it possible for prospective newspaper publishers to locate their publication centres in remote areas. It has also helped the multi-edition publications to coordinate their activities in line with their editorial and related policies.

Cost effective means of production enable committed persons and agencies to start small scale publications catering to different communities.

What it all means is that there is an immense possibility for different kinds of arrangements to cater to the diverse and specific needs of our rural areas. It is against this backdrop that training of journalists for the rural press has to be viewed.

When we say training I assume that we are referring to it as something more than mere skills. This distinction is important for me and my colleagues in the University stream for we have always believed that while education is liberal and intended to raise the students' critical consciousness, skills are preparing the students for entry to specific jobs in the media. Without getting into any discussion over the lapses, etc. of our training programmes which have been debated extensively, it is important for us to understand that there is no ambiguity with regard to the need for training.

An important question that needs to be answered is whether there is any distinction between training for the press in general and training for the rural press. The answer is yes. There is a difference and it is manifest in three or four areas:

(a) Location of the publication centre;
(b) Demographic variables of the existing and potential readership base;
(c) Social and economic structures that are more oriented towards farming and agricultural operations;
(d) Visible caste and communal parameters; and
(e) Feudalistic patterns of concentration and display of power.

There may be many more interrelated factors which reinforce one truism. The contextual base of any press catering to, or publishing from a rural area is different. Thus, we have to recognise that mainstream press despite its good intentions and sectoral coverage cannot fully cater to the context described above. Neither do they have incentives for doing justice. However, unattractive this proposition is, the need for an alternative medium exists. (I am sure that the resource persons speaking on the scope and need for a vibrant rural press have or will amplify this).

There are two kinds of training options :

1. Training for inservice journalists.
2. Training for students aspiring to be rural journalists.

Training for Inservice Journalists

The training for inservice journalists is complex as we have to recognise that as journalists they would have certain preconceived notions about coverage for rural areas and certain resistance to training. This can be overcome by careful planning on the part of the training institution to prepare a worthwhile package. Sincere efforts should be made to do a systematic analysis of the nature of coverage being provided and their inadequacies. Attitudinal problems can be overcome by motivation techniques that explain the legitimate share of the rural areas vis-a-vis coverage. Frontier areas—such as science, agrarian reforms, political analysis, problems of the marginalized sectors and awesome gaps between promise and performance of various rural areas development programmes can be used as examples. A wealth of academic material is being generated in these areas and they can be used as source material. The propensity of the journalist to know more should be exploited in a workshop environment. It is very important that in the case of inservice journalists the training component is more in the form of a dialogue supported extensively by rich sources of information and analysis.

The purpose of this exercise is to sensitize the journalists. By this, we will be achieving the purpose of motivating the gatekeepers to have rural areas on their agenda.

A few attempts in this direction have been made. The National Institute of Rural Development (NIRD) in collaboration with the Press Institute of India (PII) organized a workshop in Hyderabad. It was intended to share the experience of correspondents and reporters. An opportunity for the reporters to interact with field level functionaries and beneficiaries of various programmes was created during the workshop. The problems recognised and which are relevant today are : availability of data and their authenticity ; infrastructural facilities; language problems; and risks and threats involved. A few suggestions were also made treating rural coverage at par with other areas; fellowships for rural reporters; training for writing on rural development and development for better presentation and promoting readership for rural news.

It is also important to point out that the scope for rural reporting and coverage is better and relevant in the Indian language press more than English. English language press can at best serve as a feedback mechanism for the bureaucracy and sensitising the elite readership towards developmental issues affecting the rural areas directly. Media analysts agree that the future for the Indian press lies mainly in the language press. The success of the district pages of *Eenadu* and *Malayala Manorama* testify to this assertion.

One of the first newspapers to apply the concept of development journalism and successfully carry it out was Kannada newspaper, *Udayavani*. Through a unique project known as — "Identify the Backward Village Experiment' this paper involved the readers in identifying a backward village and having done that it gave coverage to the issues and problems of the villages. The success of this experiment was it spawned many correspondents in the villages. The experiment has been documented in a book form and has also been reported in the press.

Much has been said about the attitude of the newspaper towards issues relevant to rural India. Critics have noted this with regard to Environmental Reporting. For example, Ramachantra Guha notes that, relatively, cricket coverage assumes greater importance than these issues. He also suggests that powerful media and their communicators can take sides. He cites the case of the sympathetic coverage of environmental issues by critiques being opposed by influential columnists of leading dailies and magazines. Three serious criticisms are levelled against the press : Issues having relevance once they cease to be newsworthy; equation of people's movements more with their leaders; almost total neglect of important work being alone better within and outside the government. This is one instance of coverage having greater relevance to the rural areas There are other areas as well.

Training for Students in Universities and Other Institutions

The second group for which a training programme can be initiated is the students enrolled in different university and non-university level programmes.

Education for journalism at the university level began more than 50 years ago. There are numerous criticisms about the programme. Yet, we can say that in whatever form the programmes exist, they all reflect a philosophy that believes in a broad based education coupled with skills. The education part of the course by providing a fairly extensive background to the evolution and practices of mass media (in this case the press) enables the student to know the merits and demerits of the existing patterns of coverage. A critique of third world communication problems and prospects sensitises the student to different issues. Developmental issues dominate such discussion and the student is prepared to understand the rural context in a systematic manner. Subsequently, they are also encouraged to pursue research.

On the skills side they are put through editing and reporting exercises in class and allowed to practise them in their laboratory journal. It is in this area that severe charges have been made that professionalisation is lacking. A few attempts have been made to improve the situation. But as Rajan points out the flexibility that the private institutions enjoy vis-a-vis payment and other facilities for professionals is absent when it comes to the University. This dissuades many professionals from entertaining any requests from the University. Luckily, some of the alumini who enjoy high professional esteem are coming forward to help us. This does not reduce the need for the Universities to have a better reward system for professionals.

At this stage it may be worthwhile for me to share my experience in directing a communications programme in a small town. Used to teaching students in a media saturated environment it took some time for me to recognise that an intense media environment and access to professionals was lacking in a small town and this was an impediment in conducting the programme. This, by itself posed a challenge and slowly we are getting over it by mapping our environment critically, which is a combination of industrial, agrarian, tribal and cottage industry. Issues related to gender justice, child labour, marginalisation of tribals, wildlife protection, rich cultural heritage dating back to the Sangam era and a very diverse tradition of agricultural practices loom larger than the routine concerns we were hitherto exposed.

Further, training here begins with the fundamentals of language skills and orientation towards talking to people. The advantage these students have is that they come from areas accessible to rural areas and many of them come from villages. They have a personal identification with many of the issues we discuss. What these students lack is an approach to individuals and institutions engaged in rural development activities. Infusing confidence to help them get over their diffidence is part of our training programme. There is also less ambiguity about the language and we are striving hard to train them in a language they are familiar with.

Initiating them to the concept of a newspaper was a first step. This was done at two levels : internship and practical training.

An opportunity for allowing the students to bring out a newspaper came when the University announced its NSS programme in a village. We siezed this opportunity and decided to bring out a wall newspaper for display each day of the camp. It was a training exercise. Without any access to resources or printing facilities, we decided to use Chart Paper resembling a standard newspaper sheet. All the stories were handwritten and illustrations were drawn. Wherever necessary and possible photographs were used. The purpose of stating this here is the necessity for identifying a constituency of readership in the rural areas. This experience was valuable in exposing the students to the type and kind of stories they should work on.

Technology is another area where we desire to have a strong foundation. The U.G.C. has proposed that newspaper publishing course can be regarded as an emerging area. We have highlighted the location of our University and its objectives of serving three districts as an appropriate context. A proposal has been sent. While awaiting the decision, I would particularly welcome any possibility that RIND may have in helping us to launch a rural based newspaper. Continuous availability of at least twenty young reporters with a motivation to work and a committed University with three foundation courses having direct relevance to rural areas is our infrastructure. RIND experience is Shimoga district of Karnataka can be emulated by us in Tirunelveli-Kattabomman, V.O.C. and Kanayakumari districts. In the mean time we are giving exposure to production techniques. For example, our laboratory journal *Abisheka Times* is being produced with the cooperation of a daily. The student editors get this matter typeset. The layout matter and design is worked out in the department. After getting the negatives from the newspapers we get it printed in a local press. I cannot say the laboratory journal fits the description of a rural newspaper completely. However, we are making an attempt to reflect some concern for the area we serve. The image of the University and its academic credentials help us in having a good rapport with the concerned agencies.

Within the framework of the university system, small towns can undertake the task of training students for the rural press. Practical considerations such as employment potential restrict our enthusiasm to have a dedicated orientation. As stated earlier, the job opportunities in English press, which may want a few graduates with an exposure to the rural context, is restricted. That leaves the Indian language press as a main option. Despite increase in circulation and adoption of new technology the investment in human resource development and personnel is not commensurate (in the language press) with the expectations of the graduates. I am referring to the Indian language press which commands a significant circulation. Here, it should be pointed out that the potential for training in service personnel is very high. At a national seminar on Trends of Journalism in Indian Languages last year, all speakers without any exception pointed out to the woeful situation in different languages. Apart from a discussion on working conditions, references were made to the compulsive need for an orientation about various issues. Adoption of various techniques to woo the potential readers, the hidden consumers have definitely revamped the priorities leaving the rural based readers to slowly get coopted. The spread of the literacy movement has augmented the issue for a medium that can cater to the neo-literates. In these days of liberalisation and increased avenues of entrepreneurship, youngsters can take to the production of rural oriented newspapers serving a few blocks or maximum a district. Non-Governmental Organizations (NGOs), consumer and citizen based activists, philanthropists, foundations and universities may be persuaded to provide the necessary cost, investment or infrastructure.

Training for the Rural Press is an investment in human resource development at the grassroot level. Media have a role in it. Nevertheless we should not forget that mere communication is not a sufficient condition for development. It cannot overcome the structural limitations engendered by vested interests. It can consciously help the people to realize their potential in negotiating the odds against them. A vibrant rural press is a facilitator in this process.

8

RURAL PRESS
A Critical Input for Rural Development

— *Vir Bala Aggarwal*

One of the principal concerns in the developing countries during the past decades has been to optimise the role of communication in rural development.

The study of the role of communication received urgent attention because of the massive deployment of the economic and human resources for development in rural areas. Whereas earlier, there has been wide spread criticism for overlooking communication as an important factor in development programmes, subsequently the approach of the "top-down" process, which assumed a one-way information flow from the official agencies to the rural population, also came to be disregarded as inadequate and flawed. This approach associated at times with poorly designed communication messages and inappropriate communication messages resulted in failure of several of the development programmes. Therefore, there can be no single track, single channel approach to the use of communication support for rural development. And certainly not so in India, essentially a pluralistic society, a country of sub-continental dimensions, with a vast population at different levels of economic, educational and cultural levels with vastly different perceptions of development.

In order to reach this massive and heterogeneous clientele, with varying levels of comprehension and appreciation of their requirements and needs, we would have to take recourse to the multi channel communication strategies; interpersonal communication, rural press, radio broadcasting and also the increasing use of television in the development process.

Rural Press

The role of Rural Press has been universally recognised by all those who are interested in development—the mass communication experts and practitioners, governments of developing countries, international organizations like UNESCO, FAO and other similar specialist bodies; as also organizations working in the areas of agriculture, family welfare, food and nutrition, adult literacy, etc. The International Commission for the Study of Communication Problems, while summarizing its recommendations, says, "The development of a community press in rural areas and small towns would not only provide print support for economic and social extension activities. This would also facilitate the production of functional literature for neo-literates as well.

In his fascinating study, *Rural Development in Asia—Meeting with Peasants,* Gilbert Etienne, gives a detailed and absorbing account of slow and silent change across the Asian villages. His travels and discussions take him to five countries of Asia—Afghanistan, Bangladesh, China, India and Pakistan and he concludes that in the rural world in Asia there have been signs of change. The enormous areas of extreme poverty in east Uttar Pradesh and Bihar are beginning to stirc. Jaisalmer in the heart of Thar desert is beginning to emerge from isolation. About China asphalt or good metal roads are no more as rare as they were during the authors first visit to China in 1953. The network has improved. The current rural development strategy of China emphasises the need to diversify the rural economy and the liberalization of system, creating more employment and income opportunities. Farmers produce more, sell more which widens the scope for trade, transportation, manufacture of handicrafts and even small, privately owned workshops.

In China rural newspapers are geared to cater to the needs of peasants and rural folks who are showing a growing interest in management techniques, science and techniques.

China has approximately 500 newspapers and journals serving the peasants. Among these are 25 national and provincial peasant newspapers, usually four-page ones, with a total circulation of 10 million copies per issue, and about 200 perfactural and country papers, mostly octavos, with a total circulation of 14.5 million copies per issue. Besides there are at least 500 rural tabloids, each with a circulation ranging from 1,000 to 100,000. There are 25 major science magazines serving the peasants published by government agricultural agencies, colleges, research institutes, associations for rural science and technology and press and publication organizations they have a total annual circulation of 20 million copies, each ranging from 10,000 to as many as 600,000 copies per issue.

Likewise in India, the rural press and particularly agricultural reporting has several shining examples of its credit which would do proud to any institution. Rural newspapers and magazines, apart from agricultural reporting in the big dailies from metropolitan cities have done a lot in creating and sustaining interest on rural topics. "Our Village Chhatera", in the *Hindustan Times,* is one of the best documented rural feature series brought out in the Indian press. Several universities, cooperative societies and even individuals have done pioneering work in this direction. They have used this medium for conveying the message of improved agricultural technology to the farmers, livestock keepers, home-makers, etc. In the area of rural reporting newspapers in Kerala have done remarkably well. In his paper, "The agricultural scene—the forgotten factor". Mammen Mathew, Editor, *Malayala Manorama,* pointed out that his own paper *(Malayala Manorama)* and *Mathru Bhumi* were the first newspapers in the country to start a farm feature. They allot one page every week exclusively for this. Other similar papers are now following suit.

What is needed is to make rural press relevant to the Indian situation. It has to encompass in itself the Indian rural life in all its aspects. The agricultural reporter shall be in touch with day-to-day life problems of the common man—a small scale or a marginal farmer, rural artisan, village school teacher. Its subjects would include profile of an artisan, success story of a farmer, problems faced in the marketing of agricultural produce, social superstitions and taboos inhibiting the economic growth and productivity. Such kind of rural press shall not only mirror the true life in the Indian villages, but shall also provide a different perspective and frame of reference for the planner and policy maker. The rural press should serve as the information centre about various schemes, plans, projects and facilities available like credit, seed, fertilizer. No individual is really indifferent to reports of births marriages, deaths, sports and successes in his community. There is always some interest in weather forecast reports, purchase and sale of livestock, new development projects like construction of a new road or a bridge in the village. The rural press which basically is grassroot journalism shall cater to all this.

Training Programmes for Rural Journalists

Training programmes for workers in rural development projects like village level workers in communication methods and those of communication practitioners in rural development would go a long way in creating the much needed mutual appreciation of both the aspects. Since, with the expansion of the print media the problems of staff training and recruitment are getting bigger every year, inhouse training should be organised by the newspapers, besides formal training in journalism schools. An appreciation course in rural problems, preferably a rural institute on an agricultural university would go a long way in redressing this deficiency. A Consultancy Service for the rural press or for those national newspapers who want to report on rural problems, would fulfil the objective in a large measure. It has also been observed that the personnel working in the rural press lack adequate training required to handle their multi-facted responsibilities. They lack not only adequate editorial ability, but also the perspective necessary to manage various aspects of a newspaper. Rural papers also lack balance—the papers coming out from government or semi-government organizations avoid giving community or political news and thereby fail to create broad interest in the reading public. Training would help the rural journalists not only to acquire the perspective of complete newspaper, but also to evolve an ideal editorial mix.

With the increasing percentage of literate rural population, level of general awareness going up in the country and expansion of media channels, Rural Press can certainly fill in the hiatus which at present exists at various levels between the development bureaucracy, agricultural scientists, political leadership and the farming community. Given sustained efforts, innovative approach and training opportunities, it would not be difficult to build a cadre of journalists who could appropriately meet the communication requirement of rural population.

9

प्रसारण माध्यम और ग्रामीण कार्यक्रम

– संजीव भानावत

ELECTRONIC MEDIA AND RURAL PROGRAMMES

— Sanjeev Bhanawat

The paper, Electronic Media and Rural Programmes, recapitulates briefly the rural development programmes relayed through Akashvani and Doordarshan. Some of these programmes are covered by Farm and Home Unit of Akashvani and Krishi Darshan in the Indian television. Dr. Bhanawat has pointed out that since television programmes are primarily entertainment and film based, meant largely for urban audience, these have not been able to establish proper ambience and dialogue with the rural population. There is, therefore, an imperative need to revamp the quality and emphasis of these programmes.

भारत जैसे विकासशील देश के ग्रामीण विकास में प्रसारण माध्यमों की विशेष भूमिका है। ग्रामीण विकास से मुख्य अभिप्राय ग्रामीण जीवन के स्तर में सुधार से लेकर लोगों को सामाजिक, राजनीतिक, आर्थिक तथा सांस्कृतिक दृष्टि से समुन्नत बनाना है। स्वतन्त्रता प्राप्ति के लगभग पांच दशक बाद भी आज हमारे देश के अनेक ऐसे क्षेत्र हैं जो जीवन की न्यूनतम आवश्यकताओं के लिए भी संधर्ष कर रहे हैं। इन क्षेत्रों के लोग राष्ट्र की मुख्य धारा के साथ अभी तक नहीं जुड़ सकें हैं। रूढ़िग्रस्त परम्पराओं से जकड़ा इनका समाज अभी तक आधुनिक विकास एवं उत्पादन की नबीनतम तकनीक के लाभों से वंचित है। ग्रामीण क्षेत्रों तक प्रसारण माध्यमों की तकनीकी दृष्टि से तो पहुंच है किन्तु व्यावहारिक दृष्टि से इन माध्यमों को अभी लम्बी मंजिल तय करनी है।

हमारे देश के प्रसारण। माध्यगों की शुरूआत काफी पहले हो गयी थी। भारत

में रेडियो के प्रसारण के प्रारम्भिक प्रयास जून १६२३ में शुरू हो गये थे जब निजी स्तर पर बम्बई में रेडियो क्लब की स्थापना की गयी। विधिवत रेडियों प्रसारण 'इंडियन ब्राडकास्टिंग कम्पनी' की स्थापना के साथ हुआ। इस कम्पनी का उद्घाटन २३ जुलाई १६२७ को बम्बई में तत्कालीन ब्रिटिश वायसराय लार्ड इरविन ने किया। इस कम्पनी की असफलता के बाद १ अप्रैल १६३० को प्रसारण क्षेत्र पर सरकार ने 'इंडियन स्टेट ब्राडकास्टिंग सर्विस' के माध्यम से सीधा नियन्त्रण कर लिया। आज आकाशवाणी के विविध केन्द्रों का जाल सारे देश में फैल चुका है। सूचना और प्रसारण मंत्रालय को १६६३–६४ की वार्षिक रिपोर्ट के अनुसार ३१ दिसम्बर १६६३ तक भारत में आकाशवाणी के नेटवर्क में १६२ प्रसारण केन्द्र थे। १६२ प्रसारण केन्द्रों के माध्यम से आकाशवाणी आज लगभग पूरे देश तक पहुंच गयी है।

भारत में दूरदर्शन का प्रारम्भ १५ सितम्बर १६५६ को नई दिल्ली केन्द्र से हुआ। ३१ दिसम्बर १६६३ तक दूरदर्शन ३१ कार्यक्रम निर्माण केन्द्रों तथा ५६२ ट्रांसमीटरों की सहायता से देश के लगभग ८४ प्रतिशत लोगों तक अपने कार्यक्रम पहुचाने में सक्षम हो गया है। इस प्रकार भारतीय दूरदर्शन ने विश्व के प्रमुख टेलीविजन संगठनों में अपना विशेष स्थान बना लिया है।

सन् १६३८ में पं. जवाहर लाल नेहरू के नेतृत्व में बनाई गयी राष्ट्रीय नियोजन समिति ने प्रसारण के चार मुख्य कार्य माने हैं–

१. समाचार और उपयोगी सूचनाओं का संकलन और प्रसारण
२. प्रौढ़ शिक्षा और ग्रामीण अज्ञान के विरूद्ध संघर्ष
३. राज्य द्वारा प्रचार
४. मनोरंजन

इस समिति ने प्रसारण से अपेक्षा की कि 'कृषि पशुपालन, मौजूदा राजनीतिक विचारों आदि के संबंध में लोगों को उपयोगी सूचनाएं पहुंचाई जाएं।' वस्तुतः स्वतन्त्र भारत में प्रसारण माध्यमों ने इस दिशा में अवश्य कुछ प्रयत्न किए हैं। यहां इन प्रयत्नों की ऐतिहासिक परम्परा पर दृष्टिपात किया जा रहा है।

आकाशवाणी और ग्रामीण कार्यक्रम

ग्रामीण कार्यक्रमों से हमारा यहां अभिप्राय कृषि कार्यक्रमों सहित ऐसे कार्यक्रमों से है जो देश की ग्रामीण जनता के लिए उपयोगी होते हैं। सूचना एवं प्रसारण मंत्रालय की नवीनतम रिपोर्ट के अनुसार (१६६३–६४) कृषि एवं गृह कार्यक्रम आकाशवाणी के सभी स्थानीय केन्द्रों सहित कुल ६२ केन्द्रों से प्रसारित किए जाते

हैं। कृषि एवं गृह इकाई में एक फार्म रेडियो अधिकारी, जो कृषि सूचना संचार का विशेषज्ञ होता है, एक ट्रांसमिशन एक्जीक्यूटिव (आलेख) और एक या दो फार्म रेडियो रिपोर्टर होते हैं। कृषि एवं गृह कार्यक्रमों की अवधि ५०–६० मिनट तक की होती है और ये हर रोज प्रसारित किए जाते हैं। इनका प्रसारण सुबह, दोपहर या शाम की सभाओं में होता है।

कृषि सम्बन्धी इन कार्यक्रमों में किसानों को कृषि सम्बन्धी जानकारी के साथ–साथ मौसम का हाल तथा बाजार भाव बताये जाते हैं। इसके अलावा ग्रामीण विकास से जुड़े विभिन्न संगठनों जैसे बैंक और ग्रामीण उद्योग आदि से सम्बन्धित जानकारी भी दी जाती है। इन कार्यक्रमों के तहत् ग्रामीण महिलाओं और ग्रामीण बच्चों के लिए भी कार्यक्रम प्रसारित किए जाते हैं। इनमें घर की देखभाल, ग्रामीण रोजगार, ग्रामीण श्रमिक, स्वास्थ्य और परिवार कल्याण आदि विषयों से सम्बन्धित कार्यक्रम प्रमुख हैं। कार्यक्रमों की इस श्रृंखला में कृषि विशेषज्ञों से सलाह करके सप्ताह में एक बार किसानों के पत्रों के उत्तर दिए जाते हैं। इस वर्ष से मंत्रालय ने सर्वोत्कृष्ठ कृषि एवं गृह कार्यक्रम को आकाशवाणी पुरस्काए प्रदान करने की घोषणा की है।

आकाशवाणी पर ग्रामीण कार्यक्रमों के प्रसारण का इतिहास काफी पुराना है। अंग्रेजों के शासन काल में आकाशवाणी से प्रसारित कार्यक्रम शहरी आधार लिए होते थे। ये कार्यक्रम मुख्यतः शहरी जनता की अभिरूचियों और आवश्यकताओं को पूरा करते थे। स्वतन्त्रता के बाद देश में अनाज का संकट गहराया। इस संकट का मुकाबला करने के लिए "अधिक अन्न उपजाओ" का नारा दिया गया। उसी दौरान ग्रामीण कार्यक्रमों में कृषि सम्बन्धी कार्यक्रमों को प्रमुखता दी जाने लगी।

वस्तुतः ग्रामीण जनता के विकासार्थ तथा उन्हें देश की विकास योजनाओं के बारे में शिक्षा देने की दृष्टि से आकाशवाणी के ग्रामीण कार्यक्रमों का महत्वपूर्ण योगदान रहा है। कृषि जगत के तकनीकी विकास, कृषक प्रशिक्षण, निरक्षरता निवारण आदि विषयों को आकाशवाणी ने सहज सरल रूप में ग्रामीण जन तक पहुंचाने तथा उनमें सामाजिक चेतना जागृत करने का कार्य किया। आकाशवाणी में फार्म और गृह यूनिट (Farm and Home Unit) सन् १९६६ में प्रारम्भ किया गया था। आकाशवाणी से ग्रामीण कार्यक्रमों का औपचारिक प्रसारण प्रायः प्रसारण के आरम्भिक वर्षों में ही शुरू हो गया था। इलाहाबाद के कृषि विश्वविद्यालय ने कृषकों के लिए उपयोगी कार्यक्रमों के प्रसारणी व्यवस्था स्थानीय स्तर पर की थी। वर्तमान समय में आकाशवाणी के ग्रामीण कार्यक्रमों में मुख्य बल कृषि के क्षेत्र में जानकारी देना है।

गोविन्दवल्लभ पंत कृषि एवं प्रौद्योगिक विश्वविद्यालय, पंतनगर के कृषि संचार विभाग के श्री भुवनचन्द आकाशवाणी के कृषि कार्यक्रमों के संबंध में किए गए

अपने अध्ययन से निम्नलिखित परिणामों पर पहुंचे हैं –

१. कृषि कार्यक्रमों के लिए प्रातः काल की सेवा का समय उपयुक्त है।
२. कृषि कार्यक्रमों में जो भाषा प्रयुक्त हो रही है, उसका स्तर किसानों के शैक्षिक तथा बौद्धिक स्तर से ऊंचा होता है।
३. मौसम के पूर्वानुमान तथा कृषि समाचारों के लिए कुछ अधिक समय दिया जाना चाहिएं।
४. स्थानीय महत्व की अधिक कृषि सूचनाएं दी जानी चाहिए। ये सूचनाएं व्यावहारिक महत्त्व की होनी चाहिएं।
५. स्थानीय कार्यक्रम और स्थानीय कृषि संबंधी घटनाओं के समाचार अधिक दिए जाने चाहिएं।
६. कृषि कार्यक्रमों की अवधि आवश्यकता के अनुसार कुछ अधिक होनी चाहिए।
७. कृषि कार्यक्रमों को स्थानीय किसानों के आवश्यकता अनुसार होना चाहिए।

निश्चय ही भारतीय ग्रामीण विशेषकर कृषक के लिए आकाशवाणी के उक्त कार्यक्रमों का विशेष महत्त्व है। कृषि में विज्ञान एवं प्रौद्योगिकी के बढ़ते प्रयास और उपयोग से इन्हीं कार्यक्रमों ने भारतीय कृषकों को भलीभांति परिचित कराया है।

दूरदर्शन और ग्रामीण कार्यक्रम

भारत में दूरदर्शन का प्रारम्भ समाज शिक्षा के विकास की दृष्टि से किया गया था। प्रारम्भिक सरकारी बयानों और रिपोर्टों को उद्धृत करते हुए मेहरा मसानी ने लिखा है कि दूरदर्शन का विकास इस उद्देश्य को लेकर किया गया था कि "वह सामाजिक और आर्थिक विकास के कार्यक्रमों और उपायों" को सहारा देने का उपयुक्त साधन बने। खासतौर से यह बात कही गई कि टेलीविजन का इस्तेमाल अज्ञान और निरक्षरता से लड़ने के लिए एक हथियार के रूप में किया जाएगा, वह लोगों में समाजशास्त्रीय समस्याओं की चेतना जगाएगा और उन्हें राष्ट्रीय लक्ष्यों के प्रति जागरूक बनाएगा, वह एक नयी समाज–व्यवस्था की स्थापना के लिए भारत के प्रयत्नों में सहभागिता की भावना पैदा करेगा, वह नागरिक चेतना जगाने तथा विधि व्यवस्था, सार्वजनिक नैतिकता आदि के प्रति सम्मान पैदा करने में महत्त्वपूर्ण भूमिका निभाएगा और मनोरंजन के क्षेत्र में वह जनरूचि को उच्चतर सौन्दर्य स्तरों की ओर मोड़ेगा।

दूरदर्शन पर प्रारम्भिक कार्यक्रम एक घंटे के होते थे जो सप्ताह में दो बार

मंगलवार तथा शुक्रवार को प्रसारित किए जाते थे। इनमें से चालीस मिनट के कार्यक्रम सामुदायिक केन्द्रों के लिए समाज शिक्षा के कार्यक्रम होते थे। ग्रामीण दर्शकों के लिए "कृषि दर्शन" का प्रारम्भ २६ जनवरी १६६७ में किया गया। बीस मिनट का यह कार्यक्रम प्रत्येक बुधवार और शुक्रवार को प्रसारित किया जाता था। जुलाई १६७० से इस कार्यक्रम को सप्ताह में तीन दिन दिखाया जाने लगा। शनैः शनैः इन कार्यक्रमों की अवधि में वृद्धि होती गयी।

दूरदर्शन से सभी केन्द्र ग्रामीण निवासियों के लिए नियमित कार्यक्रमों का प्रसारण करते हैं। इन कार्यक्रमों में ग्रामीण रूचि के अनुसार मनोरंजक बातों को शामिल करने के अलावा विकास के कई अन्य पहलुओं को भी सम्मिलित किया जाता है, जैसे– परिवार कल्याण परियोजनाएं, सामुदायिक विकास, पशु–पालन, व्यावहारिक साक्षरता आदि। लेकिन मुख्य जोर कृषि पर दिया जाता है।

दूरदर्शन के प्रत्येक केन्द्र की एक ग्रामीण कार्यक्रम सलाहकार समिति होती है। इस समिति में राज्यों के सम्बद्ध विभागों के कर्मचारी, कृषि विश्वविद्यालयों तथा अन्य संस्थाओं के विशेषज्ञ तथा प्रगतिशील किसान आदि सदस्य के रूप में शामिल होते हैं।

दूरदर्शन की विकास यात्रा में उपग्रह प्रशिक्षण टेलीविजन प्रयोग (SITE) का महत्वपूर्ण योगदान रहा है। यह परियोजना १ अगस्त १६७५ को एक वर्ष के लिए शुरू की गयी थी। इस परियोजना में राजस्थान, मध्यप्रदेश, बिहार, कर्नाटक, उड़ीसा तथा आंध्रप्रदेश के लगभग २४०० गांवों में प्रतिदिन विद्यालय, कृषि तथा समाज–शिक्षा के कार्यक्रम प्रसारित किए जाते थे। इस कार्य के लिए अमरीकी उपग्रह एप्लीकेशन टेक्नोलोजी सेटेलाइट.६ ; |जै.६द्ध भारत को उपलब्ध कराया गया था। ये कार्यक्रम हिन्दी, उड़िया, तेलगु तथा कन्नड़ भाषाओं में तैयार किए जाते थे जो सम्बन्धित राज्यों में दिखाये जाते थे। बिहार, राजस्थान तथा मध्यप्रदेश के लिए ये कार्यक्रम हिन्दी भाषा में प्रसारित होते थे जबकि उड़ीसा में उड़िया, आंध्रप्रदेश में तेलगु तथा कर्नाटक में कन्नड़ भाषा में ये कार्यक्रम प्रदर्शित किए जाते थे।

साइट परियोजना की मूल कल्पना भारत के प्रख्यात वैज्ञानिक डॉ० विक्रम साराभाई की थी। कृषि सम्बन्धी जानकारी के साथ–साथ स्वास्थ्य एवं परिवार कल्याण आदि ऐसे प्रमुख शैक्षिक विषय थे जिन पर उपयोगी कार्यक्रमों का निर्माण किया गया। इस परियोजना की यह विशेषता थी कि यह अपने निर्धारित कार्यक्रम के अनुसार पूरी कुशलता के साथ पूरी हुई। अपनी कुछ कमजोरियों के बावजूद यह परियोजना भारत के ग्रामीण क्षेत्रों के दर्शकों के लिए अनूठा अनुभव था।

जोशी समिति की संस्तुतियां

६ दिसम्बर १९८२ को भारत सरकार ने देश के सामाजिक तथा आर्थिक विकास की प्रक्रिया में सहायता करने के दूरदर्शन के मुख्य उद्देश्यों को ध्यान में रखते हुए तथा सूचना, शिक्षा और मनोरंजन उपलब्ध करने के लिए प्रभावी माध्यम के रूप में कार्य करने के लिए दूरदर्शन के लिए कार्यक्रम सम्बन्धी योजना तैयार करने के लिए डॉ० पी.सी. जोशी की अध्यक्षता में एक कार्यदल गठित किया। १२ अगस्त १९८५ को इस समिति की रिपोर्ट संसद के पटल पर प्रस्तुत कर दी गयी। इस समिति ने भारत की जनता के शिक्षण, विकास, परिवार कल्याण, व्यावसायिक विज्ञापन आदि के क्षेत्र में दूरदर्शन कार्यक्रमों पर महत्वपूर्ण सुझाव दिए।

भारत जैसे विकासशील देश में ग्रामीण क्षेत्रों में जन चेतना के प्रसार और विकास में जोशी समिति ने दूरदर्शन की महत्वपूर्ण भूमिका को रेखांकित किया है। इस कार्यकारी दल ने यह स्पष्ट कहा है कि गरीबी व निरक्षरता के विरूद्ध लड़ाई लड़ने तथा विकास के लिए संचार क्रांति समान रूप से तथा टेलीविजन विशेष रूप से एक माध्यम के रूप में अभी भी वैध है। किसी ने सही ही कहा है क़ि "यदि आप किसी देश तथा वहां के लोगों के बारे में जानना चाहते हैं तो वहां का टेलीविजन देखिए। यह किसी राष्ट्र के स्वरूप का दर्पण है।"

सामाजिक शिक्षा तथा विकास को बढ़ावा देने के लिए जोशी समिति ने यह सिफारिश की है कि दूरदर्शन के प्रत्येक ट्रांसमीटर में दिल्ली के कार्यक्रम रिले करने के साथ–साथ स्थानीय महत्व के कार्यक्रम बनाने तथा प्रसारित करने और सम्बद्ध भाषायी क्षेत्र में निकटतम बड़े केन्द्र के कार्यक्रम रिले करने की भी सुविधा होनी चाहिए। समिति का मानना था कि इससे हम ऐसे विकासोन्मुखी कार्यक्रम प्रसारित करने में समर्थ हो सकेंगें जो स्थानीय भाषाओं और बोलियों में होंगें तथा क्षेत्र विशेष और दर्शकों की आवश्यकताओं के अनुरूप होंगें।

इस कार्यदल ने ग्रामीण इलाकों में सामुदायिक टी.वी. सेटों की व्यवस्था करने की सिफारिश की है। कार्यदल का मानना था कि हमें एक संस्थागत ढांचा विकसित करना होगा जिसमें केन्द्रीय सरकार के सम्बद्ध मंत्रालय, योजना आयोग, राज्य सरकारों, भारतीय रिजर्व बैंक और अन्य राष्ट्रीयकृत बैंकों के प्रतिनिधियों, प्रतिष्ठित संस्थानों के ग्रामीण योजना और विकास सम्बन्धी विशेषज्ञों तथा किसान संगठनों और स्वयंसेवी एजेंसियों के प्रतिनिधियों का सहयोग लिया जाए। इस कार्यदल ने यह भी सिफारिश की कि प्रत्येक गांव के लिए कम से कम एक टेलीविजन सेट की व्यवस्था की जाए जिससे समाज के कमजोर वर्ग टेलीविजन कार्यक्रम देख सकें। एक ऐसे विशेष कार्यदल का गठन भी किया जाए जो देश के विभिन्न राज्यों के लिए सामुदायिक सेटों की व्यवस्था करने का समयबद्ध कार्यक्रम बनाये जिसमें सबसे अधिक पिछड़े और सबसे निर्धन क्षेत्रों को विशेष प्राथमिकता दी जाये।

जैसा पूर्व में कहा गया कि टेलीविजन किसी राष्ट्र के स्वरूप का दर्पण होता है। इस दृष्टि से भारतीय दूरदर्शन की समीक्षा करने पर महसूस होता है कि हम अपने मूल लक्ष्यों से भटक गये हैं। भारत में टी.वी. की शुरूआत मुख्यतः सूचना और शिक्षा के उद्देश्य से की गयी थी। अब टी.वी. के लिए सूचना और शिक्षा गौण हो गये हैं तथा मनोरंजन प्रमुख हो गया। दूरदर्शन के "प्राइम टाइम" में अक्सर धारावाहिक तथा फिल्म संस्कृति पर आधारित मनोरंजक कार्यक्रमों को प्रमुखता दी जा रही है। दूरदर्शन के इन कार्यक्रमों तथा विज्ञापनों के मोहक जाल ने उपभोक्तावादी संस्कृति को जन्म दिया है। ऐसे परिवेश में ग्रामीण चेतना से सम्बन्धित कार्यक्रम निश्चित रूप से गौण हो गये हैं।

जोशी समिति के प्रतिवेदन में यह स्पष्ट कहा गया है कि "दूरदर्शन को भारतीय समाज के आधारभूत वर्गों–ग्रामीण किसानों, कारीगरों और मजदूरों, शहरी मजदूरों, निम्न मध्यम वर्ग के लोगों तथा बुद्धिजीवियों और महिलाओं, खासकर विभिन्न समस्याओं और तनावों से जूझ रही गांनों तथा कस्बों की महिलाओं, भारत के विभिन्न भागों में विकास के विभिन्न दौरों से गुजर रहे और विविध रंगी विरासत किन्तु असुरक्षित भविष्य लिए जनजातीय लोगों और परिवर्तनशील समाज में पीछे तथा आगे दोनों दिशाओं में देख रहे, भारत के भविष्य की आशा और संभावना के प्रतीक और विकास प्रगति की जटिल समस्याओं से घिरे बच्चों की बदलती हुई जीवन पद्धतियों और समस्याओं को अवश्य प्रस्तुत करना चाहिए।"

इस परिप्रेक्ष्य में भारतीय प्रसारण माध्यमों का मूल्यांकन करने पर प्रतीत होता है कि इन प्रसारण माध्यमों पर प्रसारित कार्यक्रम मुख्यतः शहरी आधार लिए होते हैं। संभवतः इसी कारण ग्रामीण जनों के लिए प्रसारित कार्यक्रम उनसे सीधे संवाद स्थापित नहीं कर पाते हैं। कृत्रिम से प्रतीत होने वाले सेटों पर बैठे हुए "शहरी विशेषज्ञ" जब ग्रामीणों की स्थानीय बोली के बजाय अपनी परिष्कृत और मंजी हुई भाषा में उपदेश देने का प्रयत्न करते हैं तो ग्रामीण जन उस कार्यक्रम के साथ तादात्म्य स्थापित नहीं कर पाते।

इस प्रसारण माध्यमों पर इस तरह के प्रयत्न किए जाने चाहिएं जिसमें भारतीय ग्रामीण जीवन के बदलते स्वरूप का चित्र स्पष्ट हो सके। यदि साहित्यिक विधाओं के माध्यम से एक साहित्यकार हमारे आंचलिक जीवन की गहराई और सार्थकता के साथ पाठकों के सम्मुख प्रकट करने में सक्षम हो सकते हैं तो क्यों नहीं हमारे प्रसारण माध्यमों में कार्यरत सृजनधर्मो प्रस्तुतकर्ता ऐसे कार्यक्रम तैयार करें जिनमें वह ग्रामीण जीवन को सार्थक ढंग से व्यक्त कर उसे राष्ट्र की मुख्य जीवन धारा में जोड़ सकने में सक्षम हों। निश्चित रूप से हमें दूरदर्शन और आकाशवाणी को अल्पविकास, गरीबी, असगानता तथा निरक्षरता के विरूद्ध संघर्ष के सशक्त माध्यम के रूप में विकसित करना होगा।

10

लघु समाचार पत्र : स्थिति एवं अपेक्षाएं

– अशोक चतुर्वेदी

SMALL NEWSPAPERS
Perspective and Prospects

— Ashok Chaturvedi

Of late, there has been a proliferation of small newspapers in the country. Although the number of small newspapers has vastly increased, their circulation has, however, largely remained stagnent. These papers have also not been able to improve the quality of reporting because of lack of facilities in the rural areas, and financial constraints prevent these papers from subscribing to the newsagency services. Consequently these papers have not been able to create a niche for themselves either in the local area in which they operate or establish rapport with their readers. The paper offers useful suggestions to the reporters and editors of small papers so that these could meet the objectives with which they were started.

विश्व के अन्य देशों की तरह हमारे देश में भी हजारों बहुत छोटे–छोटे समाचार पत्र प्रकाशित होते हैं। यद्यपि अधिकतर समाचार–पत्र प्रान्तीय राजधानियों या जिला मुख्यालयों से प्रकाशित होते हैं परन्तु अन्य व्यावसायिक रूप से विकसित व अन्यथा कारण से महत्त्वपूर्ण स्थलों से प्रकाशित होने वाले समाचार पत्रों की संख्या भी कम नहीं है। आज समाचार पत्र प्रकाशन ने एक उद्योग का रूप ले लिया है और समाचार–पत्र के प्रकाशन का मुख्य व प्राथमिक उद्देश्य धनोपार्जन है। यह बात छोटे बड़े सभी समाचार पत्रों पर लागू होती है। हम यहाँ उन समाचार पत्रों की बात नहीं कर रहे हैं जो अपवाद स्वरूप विशेष उद्देश्यों से प्रकाशित किए जाते हैं और जिनकी संख्या अब नगण्य सी है। संस्थाओं व संगठनों के मुखपत्र आदि भी इस लेख की क्षेत्र सीमा से बाहर हैं।

लघु छोटे आकार के समाचार पत्रों की संख्या में पिछले दशक में बहुत वृद्धि हुई है। अनेक पुराने पत्र ऐसे भी हैं जो अपनी रजत, स्वर्ण या हीरक जयन्ती भी मना चुके हैं। समाचार पत्रों की संख्या में वृद्धि एवं इनके वर्षों तक निरन्तर प्रकाशित होते रहने के उपरान्त भी इन समाचार पत्रों की प्रसार संख्या में कोई उल्लेखनीय वृद्धि नहीं हुई है। इन समाचार पत्रों के विकसित न हो पाने के बहुत से कारण हैं।

भारत सरकार के अनुसार २५,००० प्रति से कम प्रसार संख्या वाले समाचार पत्र (आकार व पृष्ठ संख्या कितनी भी हो) लघु समाचार पत्रों की श्रेणी में आते हैं। सरकारी विज्ञापनों के लिए प्रसार संख्या ही को आधार माना गया है।

इन छोटे समाचार पत्रों का मूल्य कम होता है और प्रसार संख्या कम व सीमित होती है। प्रसार संख्या के सीमित व कम होने के कारण इन्हें बड़े विज्ञापनदाताओं का सहयोग भी नहीं मिल पाता है। और अधिकतर समाचार पत्र सदैव आर्थिक कठिनाई में रहते हैं। आर्थिक परेशानियों के कारण ही ये समाचार पत्र न तो पर्याप्त कर्मचारी रख पाते हैं और न ही ऐसे मुद्रण यंत्रों की व्यवस्था कर पाने में सक्षम होते हैं जिनसे अधिक संख्या में त्वरित गति से समाचार पत्रों का मुद्रण सम्भव है। आज भी, जब आफसेट मुद्रण प्रणाली का युग भारत में भी आ गया है, अधिकतर छोटे समाचार पत्रों का मुद्रण प्लेटन प्रेस (ट्रेडल) और कुछ का सिलेंडर मशीनों पर हो रहा है।

समाचार एजेंसियों की सेवाएं लेना इन समाचार पत्रों की सामर्थ्य से परे होता है फिर भी बिना कोई व्यय किए इनमें विश्व समाचार प्रकाशित किये जाते हैं। इनमें अधिकतर में राज्य स्तर या जिला स्तर का कोई संवाददाता नहीं होता, फिर भी इन के पृष्ठ राज्य व जिलों के समाचारों से भरे होते हैं। ये समाचार कुछ बड़े अखबारों से, रेडियो व टेलीविजन प्रसारणों से, विभिन्न विभागों द्वारा जारी प्रेस विज्ञप्तियों से, पुलिस नियंत्रण कक्ष से, परिचितों या अपरिचितों से सुनी हुई बातों से जुटाए जाते हैं। लघु समाचार पत्रों को रोचक बनाया जा सकता है यदि उन्हें किसी विषय विशेष की रिपोर्टिंग से जोड़ दिया जाए। दुःख कि बात यह है कि अधिकांश लघु समाचार पत्र अपने को न तो स्थानीय पाठकों से जोड़ पाते हैं और न ही स्थानीय समाज में अपनी विशेष पहचान बना पाते हैं। और इसी कारण अपनी प्रसार संख्या में वृद्धि करने में असफल रहते हैं।

आज हमारा सरोकार लघु समाचार पत्रों को रोचक व लोकप्रिय बनाने से है। लघु समाचार पत्र सदा के लिए बिना उचित आय का छोटा समाचार पत्र ही नहीं बना रह सकता है। स्थानीय समाचार पत्र को स्थानीय समाज से जोड़ने व उस समाज का एक महत्वपूर्ण अंग बनाने के लिए पत्र के प्रबन्धकों को विशेष प्रयास करने होंगे और अपनी पूरी शक्ति इस बात के लिए लगानी होगी कि पत्र

भारत के समाचार पत्रों के पंजीयक (RNI) की रपट के अनुसार १९७६ से १९८८ तक भारत में समाचार पत्रों की संख्यात्मक स्थिति निम्न प्रकार रही

Year	Dailies	Tri/Bi-Weeklies	Weekly	Others	Total
1976	875	74	3,801	8,570	13,320
1977	929	78	4,225	9,299	14,531
1978	992	81	4,564	10,087	15,814
1979	1,087	86	5,023	10,972	17,168
1980	1,173	93	5,280	11,594	18,140
1981	1,264	98	5,624	12,158	19,144
1982	1,334	103	5,898	12,602	19,937
1983	1,423	108	6,122	13,105	20,758
1984	1,609	111	6,469	13,595	21,784
1985	1,802	111	6,769	13,966	22,648
1986	1,978	119	7,147	14,372	23,616
1987	2,151	132	7,501	14,845	24,629
1988	2,281	134	7,813	15,308	25,536

समाचार पत्रों की सन्.१९८८ में भाषावार स्थिति

Languages	Dailies	Tri/Bi-Weeklies	Weeklies	Fortnightlies	Monthlies	Quarterlies	Others	Annuals	Total
Hindi	888	39	3,756	1,351	1,773	301	96	18	8,222
English	190	17	509	407	1,832	904	490	109	4,458
Assamese	8	1	34	23	31	8	6	—	111
Bengali	60	11	473	326	529	317	105	7	1,828
Gujarati	49	4	225	108	367	41	27	9	830
Kannada	132	4	218	131	299	32	10	2	828
Kasmiri	—	—	1	—	—	—	—	—	1
Malayalam	148	1	137	125	528	32	13	6	990
Marathi	158	14	438	119	366	74	33	71	1,273
Oriya	25	—	56	41	177	56	13	4	372
Punjabi	48	1	222	47	186	23	17	1	545
Sanskrit	2	—	5	1	13	11	3	—	35
Sindhi	7	—	27	8	31	4	2	—	79
Tamil	166	5	171	164	504	19	6	1	1,036
Telugu	63	2	184	166	290	17	5	1	678
Urdu	244	13	813	230	376	36	13	3	1,728
Bilingual	36	14	401	217	792	242	88	25	1,815
Multilingual	9	2	69	39	171	53	24	7	374
Others	48	6	74	32	104	57	12	—	333
Total	2,281	134	7,813	3,485	8,369	2,227	963	264	25,536

इन समाचार पत्रों का प्रकाशन स्थल के आधार पर विश्लेषण इस प्रकार है

Centre of Publication	Dailies	Tri/Bi-Weeklies	Weeklies	Others	Total
Metropolitan cities	340	28	1,040	6,046	7,454
State capitals	558	25	1,433	2,552	4,568
Union territories other than Delhi	23	1	66	205	295
Bigger cities with population of more than one lakh	855	39	2,702	3,719	7,315
Smaller towns with population less than one lakh	505	41	2,572	2,786	5,904
Total	2,281	134	7,813	15,308	25,536

शुद्ध रूप से एक स्थानीय पत्र बन जाए। यदि पत्र का प्रकाशन कुछ रचनात्मक सिद्धान्तों के आधार पर किया जाय तो कोई कारण नहीं कि प्रकाशन सफल न हो। आवश्यकता इस बात की है कि प्रबन्ध व सम्पादन के लिए उत्तरदायी व्यक्ति कल्पनाशीलता से कार्य करें।

किसी भी समाचार पत्र के प्रकाशन में उद्देश्य यह रहता है कि पाठकों को ताजा समाचारों के साथ–साथ सामयिक विषयों पर चर्चा, मनोरंजन जैसे सिनेमा, खेल, सांस्कृतिक कार्यक्रमों आदि के बारे में जानकारी उपलब्ध कराई जाए और समाज के कल्याण में भी कुछ योगदान किया जाए। समाचार पत्र एक विज्ञापन माध्यम का भी कार्य करते हैं और इसके द्वारा स्वयं के लिए संसाधन जुटाने का कार्य तो करते ही हैं, व्यवसायी वर्ग की भी सहायता करते हैं। समाचार पत्रों का एक कर्त्तव्य यह भी माना जाता है कि वे पाठकों को महत्वपूर्ण सूचनाएँ उपलब्ध कराएँ और उचित परामर्श भी दें।

एक स्थानीय पत्र को स्थानीय पाठकों में अर्जित करने के लिए सर्वप्रथम अपनी पहचान स्थानीय जनता के साथ स्थापित करनी चाहिए। सम्पादक को समाज के ऐसे किसी भी पहलू को अनदेखा नहीं करना चाहिए जिसमें स्थानीय पाठकों की रूचि हो। पत्र को स्थानीय राजनीति, राजकीय गतिविधियों, न्यायालयों, पुलिस, खेल आदि क्षेत्रों के प्रति तटस्थ भाव अपनाने की जगह इन्हें पत्र में उचित स्थान देना चाहिए। संवाददाताओं को भी रचनात्मक दृष्टि रखते हुए ऐसी स्थानीय गति–विधियों के समाचारों को प्रधानता देनी चाहिए जिनका सम्बन्ध बहुत से स्थानीय निवासियों से हो और जो उनके लिए सुखद और प्रीतिकर हों, बजाए उन गतिविधियों के जिनका सम्बन्ध कम निवासियों से हो या जो स्थानीय क्षेत्र से बाहर घटी हों।

लघु समाचार पत्रों के सम्पादक के मस्तिष्क में अपने पत्र का एक स्पष्ट चित्र होना चाहिए कि वह समाज में अपने पत्र की क्या छवि चाहता है। इसी छवि

समाचार पत्रों की सन् १६८८ में राज्यवार स्थिति

State/Union Territories	Dailies	Tri/Bi Weeklies	Week-lies	Fortnig-htlies	Month-lies	Others	Total
Andhra Pradesh	123	3	483	228	424	90	1,351
Arunachal Pradesh	—	—	—	—	—	—	—
Assam	13	5	91	35	56	29	229
Bihar	231	13	453	107	171	57	1,032
Goa	11	—	11	9	25	15	71
Gujarat	49	2	225	98	326	82	782
Haryana	22	1	175	135	124	45	502
Himachal Pradesh	4	—	28	11	31	18	92
Jammu & Kashmir	40	2	143	16	21	9	231
Karnataka	183	6	300	183	453	127	1,252
Kerala	150	2	157	138	667	126	1,240
Madhya Pradesh	167	8	832	95	160	54	1,316
Maharashtra	224	24	791	273	1,062	623	2,997
Manipur	35	3	9	10	27	17	101
Meghalaya	2	4	28	4	12	8	58
Mizoram	24	5	24	6	5	6	70
Nagaland	—	—	8	—	—	2	10
Orissa	31	-	67	45	199	111	453
Punjab	67	1	287	104	248	67	774
Rajasthan	184	4	606	488	228	89	1,599
Sikkim	—	1	—	—	—	2	3
Tamil Nadu	172	9	195	195	751	150	1,472
Tripura	14	2	45	3	9	3	76
Uttar Pradesh	324	18	1,738	419	814	251	3,564
West Bengal	101	9	567	428	825	682	2,612
Andaman & Nicobar	1	—	13	1	5	4	24
Chandigarh	21	—	44	21	77	53	216
Dadra & Nagar Haveli	—	—	1	—	—	—	1
Daman & Diu	—	—	—	1	—	—	1
Delhi	87	11	484	428	1,632	712	3,354
Pondicherry	1	1	8	4	17	22	53
Total	2,281	13	7,813	3,485	8,369	3,454	25,536

को स्थापित करने के लिए पत्र की सम्पादकीय नीति बनाई जानी चाहिए। इस नीति का पत्र से जुड़े प्रत्येक व्यक्ति को ज्ञान होना चाहिए। संवाददाताओं को यह स्पष्ट होना चाहिए कि उन्हें किस प्रकार के समाचार एकत्र करने हैं या पत्र को देने हैं। यह सर्वविदित है कि कानून कायदे से चलने वाली जनता के पास से कोई समाचार जुटा लेना कठिन है जबकि कानून तोड़ने वाले समाजकंटकों व गैर कानूनी कार्य करने वालों के क्षेत्र से बहुत आसानी से बहुत से समाचार जुटाए जा सकते हैं।

संवाददाताओं को पत्र की नीति के अनुसार समझना चाहिए कि उनके पत्र के लिए क्या समाचार है और क्या नहीं। वह सब जो संवाददाता द्वारा लिखा जाए

हमेशा समाचार नहीं होता। फिर प्रश्न उठता है समाचार क्या है? यह परिभाषित करना कि क्या बात समाचार नहीं है और क्या समाचार है अति दुष्कर कार्य है। हम साधारणतया यह कह सकते हैं कि वह सब जो उस समय बहुत से व्यक्तियों के लिए रोचक है, समाचार है। जो समाचार जितने ज्यादा व्यक्तियों की रूचि के अनुरूप होगा वह उतना ही अच्छा समाचार माना जाएगा। कोई भी विषय समय व परिस्थितियों के अनुसार समाचार हो सकता है।

लघु स्थानीय पत्रों को रोचक व लोकप्रिय बनाने के लिए उनमें स्थानीय समाचारों की प्रमुखता होनी चाहिए। इन स्थानीय समाचारों को विस्तार के साथ, पृष्ठभूमि सहित दिया जाना चाहिए। संवाददाताओं को ऐसी समाचार–कथाओं की खोज में रहना चाहिए। उन्हें ऐसे स्थानों व विषयों पर भी ध्यान देना चाहिए जिन पर साधारणतया ध्यान नहीं दिया जाता। थोड़ी सी मेहनत व अच्छे वर्णन द्वारा छोटी स्थानीय घटनाओं को भी रोचक और महत्वपूर्ण बनाया जा सकता है।

यह बात संदेह से परे है कि लघु स्थानीय समाचार पत्रों के पाठकों की रूचि बनाए रखने में स्थानीय समाचारों की मुख्य भूमिका होती है। आज जब विश्व भर में प्रत्येक क्षण समाचारों से भरा है, सम्पादक व संवाददाताओं को अपने पाठक की रूचि, आवश्यकता के साथ ही उसकी समाचार ग्रहण करने की क्षमता व सामाजिक पृष्ठभूमि को भी ध्यान में रखना चाहिए। उन्हें यह भी दृष्टिगत रखना होगा कि छोटे व स्थानीय अखबारों को महानगरीय बड़े समाचार पत्रों से प्रतियोगिता करनी पड़ती है जो आज न केवल छोटे शहरों बल्कि ग्रामीण अंचलों तक घुसपैठ कर अपनी जड़ें जमा रहे हैं।

अधिकतर लघु समाचार पत्रों के नहीं जम पाने के दो मुख्य कारण होते हैं। प्रथम तो वे अपने आपको स्थानीय जन साधारण से तादात्म्य स्थापित कर अपनी पहचान बनाने में असफल रहते हैं। द्वितीय वे स्थानीय समाचार क्षेत्रों को पहचान कर उनका दोहन नहीं कर पाते हैं। वरिष्ठ पत्रकार व प्रेस ट्रस्ट आफ इण्डिया के पूर्व संवाददाता श्री एन.एन. शास्त्री के अनुसार जिला स्तर या तहसील स्तर के संवाददाताओं को ऐसा विचार करना चाहिए कि उनका कार्यक्षेत्र एक देश समान है। और उस क्षेत्र का सर्वोच्च अधिकारी प्रधानमंत्री समान है। ऐसे ही अन्य अधिकारियों को लेना चाहिए और इसी के अनुसार अपने समाचारों की वरीयता निश्चित करनी चाहिए। चूंकि स्थानीय जनता के लिए नामों का महत्व होता है और उन्हीं से समाचार बनते हैं और स्थानीय जनता की समाचार में रूचि बनती है, समाचारों में व्यक्तियों के नाम दिया जाना भी महत्वपूर्ण है। किसी भी समारोह या गतिविधि के आयोजकों, संचालकों, भाग लेने वालों आदि व्यक्तियों को स्थानीय समाचारों व समाचार पत्रों में अधिक स्थल देने से समाचार पत्र की लोकप्रियता में निःस्सन्देह वृद्धि होगी।

पिछले वर्षों में पाठकों की रूचि के बारे में किए गए सर्वेक्षणों से पता चला है कि स्थानीय समाचार पत्रों के सर्वाधिक लोकप्रिय व प्रसार संख्या की वृद्धि के लिए महत्वपूर्ण बिन्दु स्थानीय समाचार, लेख, साक्षात्कार आदि ही रहे हैं।

इन सर्वेक्षणों के अनुसार स्थानीय समाचार स्तम्भ पाठकों की पत्र में रूचि में वृद्धि करते हैं। ७० प्रतिशत से अधिक पाठकों की रूचि अपने मन्दिर, अपने शहर, अपने अस्पताल, अपने स्थानीय इतिहास आदि के बारे में, अन्तर्राष्ट्रीय समाचारों की अपेक्षा अधिक होती है।

अधिकतर स्थानीय समाचार पत्र अपने आपको बड़े दैनिक पत्रों के अनुरूप बनाने का प्रयास करने और उनसे प्रतियोगिता करने की गलती करते हैं। हमें समझना चाहिए कि आंचलिक क्षेत्रों में कुल साक्षर जनसंख्या में ऐसे व्यक्तियों की संख्या कम होती है जिनमें अन्तर्राष्ट्रीय समाचारों की ग्राह्यता हो। बड़े शहरी दैनिक पत्र असाधारण को अधिक महत्व देते हैं, जबकि छोटे समाचार पत्रों के पाठक के लिए परिचित व विशिष्ट क्षेत्र अधिक महत्वपूर्ण होते हैं।

लघु समाचार पत्रों के संवाददाताओं को स्थानीय समाचारों व घटनाओं को अधिक महत्व देना चाहिए न कि एजेन्सी या रेडियो के राष्ट्रीय व अन्तर्राष्ट्रीय समाचारों को लघु समाचार पत्रों के संवाददाताओं व सम्पादक को अपने पाठकों की विशिष्ट मनोवैज्ञानिक स्थिति का भी अध्ययन करना चाहिए। एक महानगर में रहने वाले व्यक्ति, राज्य की राजधानी में रहने वाले व्यक्ति, अन्य शहरों में रहने वाले व्यक्ति व ग्रामीण अंचलों में रहने वाले व्यक्ति सभी की मानसिकता अलग–अलग होती है।

लघु समाचार पत्रों का एक कर्तव्य यह भी होना चाहिए कि वे अपने पाठकों को नवीनतम वैज्ञानिक खोजों, प्रशासनिक सुधारों, विकास योजनाओं व सामाजिक तथा आर्थिक परिवर्तनों आदि से भी अवगत कराते रहें। इन सब विषयों पर पाठकों की क्षमता को दृष्टिगत रखते हुए भी सामग्री का प्रकाशन किया जाना चाहिए।

संवाददाताओं को स्थानीय अदालतों, पुलिस नियंत्रण कक्ष या थाने, अस्पताल, खेल–मैदान, हाट बाजार एवं अन्य सार्वजनिक स्थानों पर जाते रहना चाहिए जहाँ पर स्थानीय सूचनाएं व समाचार मिलना अवश्यम्भावी है। सामाजिक संस्थाएं जो कुछ न कुछ गतिविधि करती रहती हैं, व्यापारिक संस्थाएं जैसे चैम्बर ऑफ कामर्स की शाखा, व्यापार मण्डल, मण्डी समिति, आदि ऐसे स्थान हैं जहां से स्थानीय समाचारों की प्राप्ति सम्भव है।

स्थानीय समाचार पत्रों की सामुदायिक विकास में एक महत्वपूर्ण भूमिका होती है और आज समय है जब इस भूमिका को निभाने के लिए इन समाचार पत्रों को आगे आना चाहिए। ऐसा करने के लिए हमें समाचार एकत्र करने के व समाचार पत्र सम्पादन की उन पारम्परिक रूढ़ियों व तरीकों से बाहर निकलना होगा जो

वर्षों पहिले बड़े समाचार पत्रों के सम्पादकों व संवाददाताओं द्वारा बनाई गई थीं। हमें यह समझना चाहिए कि शहरी व बड़े समाचार पत्रों का क्षेत्र लघु समाचार पत्रों के क्षेत्र से सर्वथा पृथक है। दोनों में कोई प्रतिस्पर्धा नहीं है। लघु समाचार पत्रों को अपनी भूमिका निभाने के लिए अपने क्षेत्र के अनुसार, अपने पाठकों की रूचि के अनुसार समाचार, लेख व समाचार कथाएं प्रकाशित करनी चाहिएं, जिससे वे स्थानीय जनता में लोकप्रिय हों व्यावसायिक रूप से सफल हों और साथ ही अपनी भूमिका सामाजिक उत्थान में उत्तरदायित्व के साथ निभा सकें।

11

ग्रामीण चेतना और पत्रकारिता

— राधेश्याम शर्मा

RURAL AWAKENING AND JOURNALISM

— Radhey Shyam Sharma

The paper underlines the increasing importance of information as a product and commodity. The Information Revolution sweeping the world, information networks and access to information have virtually changed the parameters of journalism in the contemporary world. Information is no longer a monopoly in the hands of a group of people, the affluent and the rich. During the present decades, alongwith expansion in the reach and sweep of electronic media, print media has also expanded. This is because more and more people want to know more and more about how government policies affect them and their life styles. Therefore, there is an imperative need that community newspapers continue to play the important role of establishing a link between the government and policy makers and the rural clientele it serves.

आज सभी ओर नयी चेतना दिखायी देती है। पहले औद्योगिक क्रांति एवं वैज्ञानिक खोजों ने जीवन की सारी शैली बदल दी। फिर भी दुनिया के अनेक देश उसकी चकाचौंध से बचे रहे और पुराने ढर्रे पर चलते रहे, लेकिन आज सभी ओर सूचना या जानकारी के पलक मारते एक छोर से दूसरे छोर पर पहुंचने से भी जीवन की सारी शैली बदल गयी है। पत्रकारिता और प्रचार मीडिया खासकर इलेक्ट्रानिक मीडिया ने इसमें जबरदस्त रोल अदा किया है। इसने सुदूर ग्रामीण अंचल और वनवासी अंचल तक जनचेतना जगाने में बहुत बड़ी भूमिका अदा की है।

वह दिन गये जब विश्व की बड़ी हस्ती नेपोलियन की सेंट हेलेना में मौत की सूचना उनके देश फ्रांस में दो माह बाद पहुंची थी। आज अखबार, दूरदर्शन, रेडियो, दूरसंचार, सेटेलाइट आदि के माध्यम से सूचना–क्रांति आ गयी है। निश्चय

ही विज्ञान एवं वैज्ञानिक खोज और तकनीक का इसमें महत्वपूर्ण हाथ रहा है लेकिन इस खोज की सूचना का फैलाव ही परिवर्तन का मूल कारण है।

आज कोई व्यक्ति या सरकार कोई सूचना को दबाकर नहीं रख सकते। देशों की सीमायें अब लौह आवरण से बंधी नहीं हैं। सार्वभौमिकता के लौह आवरण टूट गये हैं, बर्लिन की दीवार टूट गयी है, बनावटी सीमायें टूट गयीं। यह सब सूचना क्रांति का ही नतीजा है।

इससे ग्रामीण अंचल भी तेजी से प्रभावित हो रहा है। आज का ग्रामीण दुनिया की उन्नत खेती, रहन–सहन, नयी तकनीक के इस्तेमाल, ऊंचे जीवन स्तर के प्रति बेखबर या उदासीन नहीं है। वह भी अब सूचना–क्रांति से प्रभावित होकर बेहतर जिंदगी जीने के लिए उत्सुक है।

अब किस्मत के खेल के भरोसे रहने, खाद डालने से फसल जलने, पानी से बिजली निकाल ली इसलिए सिंचाई नहीं करने, दूध नहीं बेचने, खेती व दूध की पैदावार नहीं बढ़ाने, बदन पर कम कपड़े रखने की पुरातन धारणाओं से ग्रामीण जीवन आगे निकल गया है। उन्नत खेती, ज्यावा उत्पादन, मवेशियों की बेहतर व्यवस्था, उनके इलाज, खेती में मशीनों के उपयोग के प्रति वह आज दकियानूसी नहीं है। वह आज सब सुन रहा है और देखकर अपना भला–बुरा समझ रहा है। अब फसल की कीमत के प्रति वह ज्यादा सजग है और अपने हकों के प्रति भी। ग्रामीण अंचल में नयी चेतना का श्रेय सूचना–क्रांति को है। पत्रकारिता ने इस अंचल को जगाया और संचार साधनों ने इसे तेजी से दौड़ने का रूप दिया। पत्रकारिता से अंधविश्वास, दकियानूसी ढर्रे और जड़ता का शिकंजा ढीला हुआ। ग्रामीण अंचल प्रगति एवं विकास की जरूरत के प्रति सजग हुआ। पहले तो वह इसके प्रति उदासीन था। निश्चय ही रेडियो व दूरदर्शन ने इसे तेज गति दी, परंतु पत्रकारिता के ठोस योगदान व पृष्ठभूमि तैयार करने के योगदान को स्वीकार करना होगा।

आज का युग सूचना का युग है। युग के लिए पहले मध्य–युग, पुनर्जागरण (नवजागरण), सुधार जैसे विशेषण इस्तेमाल होते थे। अब नामकरण के लिए कोई इतिहासकार जरूरी नहीं है।

इस परिवर्तन के प्रमाण सब तरफ मौजूद हैं। आज सारी दुनिया इलेक्ट्रानिक जाल में बुनी हुई है जिसके द्वारा खबरें, आंकड़े (सही या गलत–अच्छे या बुरे) पलक मारते एक छोर से दूसरे छोर पर पहुंच जाते हैं। इस जाल के द्वारा बड़े पैमाने पर सूचना का अत्यधिक तेज गति से फैलाव हो रहा है, उससे बदलाव (कायाकल्प) की गति बढ़ी है और दुनिया की कार्यशैली भी बदल रही है। कार्यशैली का यह बदलाव उतना ही व्यापक है, जितना औद्योगिक क्रांति के दौरान हुआ था। औद्योगिक क्रांति ने समाज व्यवस्था, शासन व्यवस्था, पुरानी जकड़न को

तोड़कर जीवन की शैली ही बदल दी। सामाजिक एवं राजनीतिक व्यवस्थायें भी उससे प्रभावित हुईं। नये राजनीतिक एवं जीवन दर्शन, अर्थव्यवस्था के नये चिंतन एवं मापदंड उभरे। इससे नये टकराव भी आये लेकिन जनजीवन की गति तो तेज हुई ही।

इससे सरकार और नागरिक, एक सार्वभौम सरकार और दूसरी सार्वभौम सरकार, कम्पनियों और उनके नियंत्रकों के आपसी रिश्तों में बदलाव आ रहा है। पहले की तरह कोई प्रभावशाली व्यक्ति अब नागरिक को नहीं देख रहा है बल्कि अब नागरिक की निगाह प्रभावी व्यक्ति पर है। अब तो धन किससे निर्माण होता है, इसकी अनुभूति में भी नाटकीय बदलाव आया है। आज भौतिक पूंजी से बौद्धिक पूंजी तुलनात्मक दृष्टि से ज्यादा महत्वपूर्ण हो गयी है क्योंकि उससे भौतिक पूंजी कम समय में कई गुना ज्यादा बढ़ सकती है।

आज धन का नया स्त्रोत पदार्थ की बजाय वह सूचना एवं ज्ञान है जिसका उपयोग मूल्य पैदा करने में होता है। आज धन की तलाश मुख्यतः सूचना की तलाश करना और उसका उपयोग उत्पादन के माध्यमों में करना है।

एक जटिल साफ्टवेयर कार्यक्रम जिससे अरबों रूपये कमाये जा सकते हैं, उसे लिखने की महारत रखने वाला व्यक्ति किसी भी हवाई अड्डे या देश की सीमा पर कस्टम अधिकारी को यह कहते हुए बेरोक–टोक बाहर जा सकता है कि उसके पास टैक्स योग्य सामान घोषित करने के लिए कुछ नहीं है।

सूचना–अर्थव्यवस्था किसी भी इलाके को नियंत्रित करने के पुरस्कार के महत्व को कम कर देती है। इससे किसी इलाके को नियंत्रित करने के बाद उसके साधनों के दोहन के बाद का मूल्य भी कम हो जाता है। कई जगह खदानों से खुदायी अब घाटे का सौदा बन गयी है। खनिज की जगह दूसरे पदार्थ ले रहे हैं। प्लास्टिक व सिंथेटिक ने नयी क्रांति ला दी है। लोहे का व धातु का उपयोग घट गया है।

बहुत से देशों ने खूनी–युद्ध से किसी इलाके को जीता तो वे आज उनके लिए फायदे का सौदा बनने की बजाय बोझ बन गये। बहुत से प्राकृतिक साधन जो सीमा के अंदर थे, उनकी जगह अब सिंथेटिक चीजें ले रही हैं। यह तो दिमाग से ही पैदा हुई चीज है। जो सीमायें पहले देश की सुरक्षा का काम करती थीं अब उनमें बहुत से छिद्र हो गये हैं, जिनसे बहुत से आंकड़े और जानकारी छनकर बेरोक–टोक दूसरी जगह पहुंच जाती है। चीन ने जिस तेजी से पश्चिमी तकनीक को स्वीकार किया वह एक बड़ा उदाहरण है। सूचना–क्रांति ने रक्तिम क्रांति के रूख को बदल दिया पुराने राजनीतिक दर्शन व राजनीतिक प्रणालियां सूचना–क्रांति से उत्पन्न समाज जीवन में बेमानी होती लगती हैं।

एक विद्वान की राय में क्रांति तब तक नहीं होती, जब तक कि लोगों को

यह अहसास नहीं होता कि उनकी जीवन–शैली का कोई दूसरा विकल्प भी है। यह विकल्प ध्यान में लाना सूचना–क्रांति का काम है। दुनिया के कई हिस्सों में पहले सरकारी नीति के खिलाफ जो भी चिंतन होता था, उस पर सख्ती से नियंत्रण होता था। सरकारें अपनी नीति व विचारधारा लादे रखना चाहती थीं। दूसरी राजनीतिक विचारधारा या प्रणाली की जानकारी आना मुश्किल था। आज सेटेलाइट की मदद से ऐसे विकल्पों की जानकारी ट्रांजिस्टर की मदद से दूर जंगलों तक पहुंच रही है और दूरदर्शन की मदद से सारी दुनिया में पहुंच रही है। खेल, झोंपड़ी और झुग्गी में भी ट्रांजिस्टर फिल्मी गानों के साथ ही सूचनायें पहुचाने का बड़ा काम कर रहा है। केबल टी.वी. के कारण आज दूरदर्शन पर सरकारी नियंत्रण बेमानी हो गया है। तंजानिया की सरकार बरसों तक दूरदर्शन पर शिकंजा जमाये रही लेकिन सूचना–क्रांति के कारण वह नियंत्रण हटाना पड़ा।

जो सूचना तकनीकें मुक्ति की यह खबरें तेजी से दूसरी जगह पहुचाती हैं, वह तेजी से ऐसे हालात बना रही हैं जिसे सार्वभौमिकता का धुंधलका कहा जा सकता है क्योंकि अपने नागरिकों के खिलाफ और दूसरे नागरिकों के खिलाफ सत्ता के पूर्ण अधिकार को अकेले इस्तेमाल करने का अधिकार धीरे–धीरे कमजोर पड़ रहा है। सूचनायें मिलने पर लोगों को दबाकर रखना मुश्किल होता है।

इसका अर्थ यह नहीं है कि राष्ट्र की सत्ता लुप्त हो जायेगी। हकीकत यह है कि हम देखेंगे कि आगे चलकर बहुत से देश बन गये हैं। कई बड़े देश बिखरकर नये देशों का उदय क्या बताता है? यही कि सार्वभौमिकता की पकड़ एवं भावना ढीली पड़ रही है।

१७ वीं शताब्दी में श्री बारूच स्पिनोजा ने सूचनाओं के प्रवाह के कारण समाजों के नये बनते आकारों पर टिप्पणी करते हुए, उसे इन शब्दों में व्यक्त किया था, "राज्यसत्ता का अंतिम कार्य लोगों पर प्रभुत्व जमाना या उन्हें भय द्वारा सीमित करना नहीं, बल्कि व्यक्ति को भय से, मुक्त करना है, ताकि वह पूरी सुरक्षा से खुद को या पड़ौसी को बिना कोई आघात पहुंचाये जिन्दा रहकर काम कर सके। राज्य का अंत वास्तव में मुक्ति है।"

हम अनुभव से जान चुके हैं कि आजादी रोग का ऐसा कीड़ा है, जिसको मारने की कोई दवा नहीं है। आज यह कीड़ा इलेक्ट्रानिक माध्यम के जाल द्वारा सारी दुनिया में फैल गया है और उन इलाकों में भी फैल गया है, जो पिछले दिनों बेहतर जीवन शैली के ज्ञान की जानकारी से या उसकी उम्मीद से भी कोसों दूर थे। यह प्रक्रिया अब गति पकड़ चुकी है और इसे अब उल्टी दिशा में नहीं मोड़ा जा सकता क्योंकि जिस तकनीक पर वह आधारित है वह कहीं दूर नहीं चली जायेगी। सूचना–क्रांति ने मुक्ति की भावना को मजबूत किया है। आप जागरूक व्यक्तियों को ज्यादा दिन तक दबाकर नहीं रख सकते। सूचना या जानकारी उसके

आत्म–विश्वास को मजबूत बनाती है।

प्रसिद्ध पत्रकार माइकल जे ओ' नील ने कहा था, "आज की दुनिया बीते काल की यादों के आधार पर फिर से नयी नहीं बनायी जा सकती। भविष्य के मार्ग पर कोई यू–टर्न (एकदम विपरीत दिशा में मोड़) नहीं होता। बीते दिनों में सूचना पहुंचाने का कोई विश्वव्यापी जाल नहीं था, लेकिन आज सारी दुनिया अपनी शक्ति को समझती है। १६८८ में प्रेस के प्रदर्शनकारी इस बात को अच्छी तरह समझते थे, इसलिए वहां तैनात पुलिस को वे हिम्मत के साथ कह सके कि "सावधान सारी दुनिया तुम्हें देख रही है।" और यह हकीकत थी। इसलिए पुलिस ज्यादती करने से सहम गयी। दूरदर्शन का यह चमत्कार है।

आज के युग में यह असंभव बात है कि नेपोलियन जैसे विश्वविख्यात महारथी की एक द्वीप में मई माह में मृत्यु हो और उसकी खबर दो माह बाद जुलाई में उसके देश फ्रांस में पहुंचे यदि आज ऐसा हो तो तूफान आ जाये।

आज हम सारी दुनिया को इस दृष्टि से देखते हैं, मानो हम विश्वव्यापी प्रक्रिया के हिस्से हैं। आज परिवर्तन की जो तीव्र गति हम स्वास्थ्य की चिंता से लेकर हथियारों की दौड़ तक देख रहे हैं वह सब सूचना–क्रांति और उसकी तकनीक से ही संभव हो सका है।

पहले सूचना या ज्ञान पर मुठ्ठी भर लोगों का या समूहों का एकाधिकार होता था। वह एकाधिकार धीरे–धीरे टूट चुका है, जिसका समाज पर व्यापक असर हुआ है। आज आम आदमी भी काफी कुछ जानता है।

अब सारे ज्ञान, जीवन दर्शन या पूंजी का ठेका एक व्यक्ति या एक समूह का नहीं रह गया है। हर व्यक्ति ज्ञान पाना, जानकारी रखना और पूंजी अर्जित करना अपना हक समझता है। उसके लिए प्रयास भी करता है। बैंकों, सहकारी बैंकों के अलावा शिक्षा, सूचना–क्रांति एवं जागरूकता ने यह स्थिति बनायी है। लियोन मार्टेल के शब्दों में "मुझे ऐसा दिखायी दिया है कि सूचना अब समाज का बदलाव करने में ऊर्जा का स्थान ले रही है।" ऊर्जा का पहले जो महत्व था, आज वह महत्व सूचना का है।

कम्प्यूटर और दूरसंचार का मेल होने से तो सूचना अब प्रकाश की गति से असंख्य लोगों तक पहुंचने लगी है। इससे चूंकि ज्ञान का विकेन्द्रीकरण होता है तो सत्ता का भी विकेन्द्रीकरण होता है। लोगों की जानकारी होने से सत्ता या ज्ञान का केन्द्रीयकरण आज संभव नहीं है। जानकारी के स्त्रोत एवं दायरे भी बढ़ गये हैं।

जब सेटेलाइट के कारण सूचनायें फोन या अन्य साधनों से एक से दूसरे छोर पर पहुंच जाती हैं तब सरकार भी कोई जानकारी अपनी जनता से छुपाकर नहीं रख पाती और यह एक तरह से सत्ता का हस्तांतरण है। आज गांव–गांव

तक फोन पहुंच गया है। एस.टी.डी. मौजूद है। बिजली या नयी तकनीक के प्रति आज ग्रामीण उदासीन नहीं है।

नयी बौद्धिक खोज से शारीरिक श्रम कम होता है। काम की गति बढ़ती है। वह कई गुना बड़ा हो सकता है। इसका असर भी व्यापक होता है।

चिकित्सा ज्ञान की जानकारी ने ग्रामीण क्षेत्रों एवं वनवासी इलाकों के नीम–हकीमों के और झाड़–फूंक करने वाले ओझाओं के धंधे और ताकत को ध्वस्त कर दिया। यही नयी जानकारी पहुंचने का ही नतीजा है। इसका असर जीवन शैली पर भी पड़ा है। अब ग्रामीण भी इलाज के लिए दौड़ता है। भाग्य के या झाड़–फूंक के भरोसे वह नहीं रहता। ज्ञान को काम में लगाया जाए तो धन का मूल्य पैदा होता है। अब गांव में भी दवा उपलब्ध है। चिकित्सक भी वहां पहुंच गये हैं। अब ग्रामीण व्यक्ति इलाज के प्रति सजग है। वह इस व्यवसाय से भी जुड़ गया है।

ज्ञान का अर्थ है– "तथ्य से अवगत होना, सचाई, हकीकत या सिद्धांत से अवगत होना, जैसा कि अध्ययन या खोज द्वारा ज्ञान से अवगत होना।" इस ज्ञान का उपयोग काम में या धन के उत्पादन में भी हो सकता है। यानी ज्ञान ही अंततः काम में मूल्य का स्त्रोत है। जानकारी से एक चीज के ज्यादा फायदे, ज्यादा लोग ले सकते हैं।

उदाहरण के लिए जंगल में भागता खरगोश धन नहीं है, परंतु जब शिकारी द्वारा उसे प्राप्त सूचना पर अमल होता है तो कैसे उसे पकड़ना, कैसे तीर या भाला फेंकना, भाला–तीर कैसे बनाना–जब यह सब तकनीक शिकारी इस्तेमाल करता है तो वह खरगोश धन में बदल जाता है। वह शिकारी या उसके परिवार के लोगों के लिए भोजन बन जाता है। खरगोश पकड़ना व्यवसाय बन जाता है। फिर खरगोश प्राणि–घर, प्रयोगशाला या घर में पालतू के बतौर सप्लाई होने लगता है। शिकार एक उद्योग बन जाता है।

यही बात खेती, उद्योग आदि पर लागू होती है, खरगोश को पकाने के तौर–तरीके अर्थव्यवस्था का हिस्सा बनते हैं–तंदूर में पकाया जाए या किसी मशीन में। फिर ये तीर, भाले, गोली, शिकार की नयी तकनीक व तौर–तरीके नयी व्यवस्था, अर्थव्यवस्था को जन्म देते हैं। ऐसे ही घटनायें नये व्यवसाय व धन को बढ़ावा देते हैं।

नयी व्यवस्था से ग्रामीण अंचल की जीवन शैली बदली है। कई समस्याओं का अंत हुआ है और कई समस्यायें विकराल बनी हैं जिसके हल के लिए नयी–नयी सूचनाओं की आंधी आ रही है। नयी जानकारी से ग्रामीण के समय की बर्बादी खत्म होकर समय को उत्पादन में बदलने के मार्ग खुले हैं। एक से अधिक फसल, वाणिज्य फसल, डेरी उत्पादन, ग्रामोद्योग को बढ़ावा मिला है।

खेती और उद्योगों के विकास, ग्रामीण अंचल के आर्थिक विकास ने भी ग्रामीण अंचल में पुनरूत्थान की भावना को जगाया है। इसमें राजनीति का भी कुछ योगदान रहा है, लेकिन असली रोल मेरी राय में सूचना–क्रांति का रहा है। इससे ग्रामीण अंचल में बदलाव की और आगे बढ़ने की ललक पैदा हुई है। वह जीवन के सभी क्षेत्रों में अब अपना स्थान बनाना चाहता है। जीवन स्तर के सुधार के प्रति भी वह सजग है और हकों के प्रति भी।

निश्चय ही शिक्षा के फैलाव ने भी ग्रामीण जीवन में पुनरूत्थान की भावना एवं जागृति पैदा करने में महत्वपूर्ण भूमिका अदा की है लेकिन इसका भी मुख्य श्रेय सूचना–क्रांति को है। इससे ही शिक्षा की भूख जगी है। इस सूचना, नयी जानकारी, नयी खोज एवं नयी तकनीक ने और इनके सफल प्रयोग के साथ–साथ इन सफल प्रयोगों की सूचना पहुंचाने के काम ने भी बहुत बड़ा रोल अदा किया है। पत्रकारिता इसका महत्वपूर्ण माध्यम रही है। लोगों की चेतना जगाने, उन्हें जागरूक करने, उनका आत्मविश्वास जगाने और अपने उत्थान के प्रति सजग करने में पत्रकारिता से प्राप्त सूचना का बड़ा रोल रहा है।

आज भी इस जागृति को सही दिशा देने एवं उसे सोद्देश्य बनाने में पत्रकारिता महत्वपूर्ण रोल अदा कर सकती है और कर रही है। लोग दबाव एवं दासता के भाव से मुक्त हुए हैं। इस सूचना क्रांति से जहां सजगता आयी है वहीं कहीं–कहीं बिखराव भी आया है। कहीं लोग आत्म–केन्द्रित भी हुए हैं। घर बैठे जानकारी मिलने से आपसी मेलजोल में कमी आयी है और सत्ता का शिकंजा कमजोर पड़ने से सार्वभौमिकता का शिकंजा ढीला पड़ने से कई देशों की सीमायें उतनी पुख्ता नहीं रही हैं। इससे असुरक्षा बढ़ी है। उनमें भी बिखराव आया है। स्थानीय भावनायें, क्षेत्रीयता और वर्गगत भावनायें भी प्रबल हुई हैं। जागरूकता कभी–कभी अहं को मजबूत करती है और धैर्य व सहनशीलता को कम कर देती है। नतीजे पाने की व्यग्रता भी इसका कारण हो सकती है।

सूचना–क्रांति से जहाँ आर्थिक क्रांति आयी है, वहां वर्गगत टकराव भी बढ़ा है। पत्रकारिता को इसमें रचनात्मक रोल अदा करना है। जो पिछड़ापन एवं उससे जुड़ी तकलीफ जानकारी के अभाव के कारण थीं, वह अब आक्रोश का रूप ले रही हैं। उससे नये रिश्ते, नये गणित, नफरत और प्यार के नये मापदंड बन रहे हैं। इसके लिए सही सूचना, सही तरीके से पहुंचाना जरूरी है।

लेकिन विकास के साथ विवेक भी मजबूत हो और विनाश की ओर रूख नहीं हो यह दिशा देना पत्रकारिता का काम है। इसके लिए सूचना में संतुलन एवं रचनात्मक दृष्टिकोण जरूरी है। संचार साधनों का विवेकशील उपयोग और जानकारी के साथ ज्ञान में वृद्धि का दायित्व पत्रकारिता का है हर चीज की असलियत जानने का अर्थ अविश्वास पैदा होना नहीं होना चाहिये। दुष्परिणामों

के प्रति सजगता भी सूचना–क्रांति का जरूरी अंग है। अन्याय के खिलाफ संघर्ष एवं जनान्दोलनों की सफलता में पत्रकारिता ने बहुत बड़ा योगदान दिया है। वही ग्रामीण अंचल में परिवर्तन का आधार बना। फसल के सही दामों के लिए बिखरा किसान आज सूचना–क्रांति के कारण संगठित हो सका।

ग्रामीण जीवन में बदलाव का आज का रूख भावी परिवर्तन का संकेत है। जब सजगता आयेगी तो फिर गुण–दोष के आधार पर नीर–क्षीर विवेक भी पैदा होगा। आने वाले समय में ग्रामीण अंचल को दुर्लक्ष्य करके कोई सरकार, नेतृत्व या व्यवस्था नहीं चल पायेगी। शायद इसीलिए ग्रामीण अंचल को प्रभावित करने की राजनीतिक दलों, सरकारों एवं सामाजिक संगठनों में होड़ लगी है। विश्वव्यापी शिक्षा कार्यक्रम एवं फसलों पर आधारित अंतर्राष्ट्रीय कंपनियों के उद्योग भावी व्यवस्था का संकेत देते हैं।

समय के साथ पत्रकारिता के परिवेश एवं प्रभाव क्षेत्र में भी बदलाव आया है। पहले बड़े शहरों से ही अखबार निकलते थे और एक या दो दिन बाद पढने को मिलते थे। आज हर शहर से दर्जनों अखबार निकलते हैं। हर जिला केन्द्र, यहां तक कि तहसील–केन्द्र से भी दैनिक बड़ी संख्या में निकलते हैं। एक–एक जिले से साप्ताहिक प्रकाशित होने की संख्या सैकड़ों में है।

जाहिर है कि पाठकों की संख्या भी बढ़ी है। रेडियो और दूरदर्शन का फैलाव बहुत तेजी से हुआ है लेकिन फिर भी छपे हुए अक्षरों का महत्व कायम है। दूरदर्शन के बाद भी अखबारों की प्रसार संख्या बढ़ी है। उनके कलेवर, साजसज्जा, पृष्ठ संख्या में भारी सुधार हुआ है। रंगीन पृष्ठ, बहुरंगी मैगजीन, आकर्षक चित्रों के साथ ही कालमों की संख्या बढ़ी है।

कारण साफ है कि लोग ज्यादा से ज्यादा जानना चाहते हैं। इसलिए अखबार पढते हैं। अखबारों की संख्या बढ़ने से अब अखबार ग्रामीण अंचल में अपनी प्रसार संख्या बढ़ाने में शक्ति लगा रहे हैं। इसलिए ग्रामीण अंचल की खबरें भी ज्यादा प्रमाण में अखबारों में छपती हैं। वहां की समस्यायें, जनजीवन, लोककला, लोकगीत, लोकनृत्य, लोककथा और लोक जीवन अब अखबारों के फीचर के विषय बनते हैं। इनसे हमारा साहित्य एवं कला क्षेत्र दोनों को बल मिला है। अब इन्हें सम्मान की निगाह से देखा जाता है। ग्रामीण अंचल एवं आदिवासी अंचल का विकास और उनसे जुड़ी बातें आज अखबारों की सामग्री का विषय बनती हैं। वनवासी अंचल की खूबियों और समस्याओं के प्रति सरकार और समाज का ध्यान पत्रकारिता ने खींचा है और उन इलाकों में प्रकाश की किरण पहुंचाने में मदद की है।

इन सब कारणों से भी ग्रामों में चेतना तथा अपनी विशेषताओं के प्रति अहसास बढ़ा है। ग्रामीण अंचल की इस जागृति के साथ वहाँ के निवासियों में जागृति आयी है। उससे उनकी अपेक्षायें भी बढ़ी हैं। अब वे पिछड़पन से दबकर रहने

को तैयार नहीं हैं। वे भी सबके साथ विकास की और अपने हालात सुधारने के प्रति सजग एवं सचेष्ट हैं। लोकतंत्र में वे अपनी और अपने अंचल की कीमत पहचान गये हैं। इसमें पत्रकारिता और सूचना–क्रांति का जो योगदान रहा है वह भविष्य में भी बना रहेगा।

ग्रामीण अंचल में जो जागृति आ रही है उसे रचनात्मक दिशा एवं दृष्टि देने की बहुत बड़ी जरूरत है और यह कार्य भी पत्रकारिता के खाते में है।

जहां तक हमारे देश के ग्रामीण अंचलों का संबंध है, यहां कि स्थिति कई मायने में भिन्न है, इसलिए पत्रकारिता का रोल भी कुछ भिन्न है। ग्रामीण और वनवासी इलाकों में आवागमन के साधनों का अभाव है। आज भी हजारों गांव सड़कों से नहीं जुड़े हैं। ग्रामीण अंचल में गरीबी, पिछड़ापन, अंधविश्वास, सामाजिक पिछड़ापन एवं अशिक्षा आज भी बड़े वीभत्स रूप में हैं। इस कारण शोषण बरकरार है और न्याय भी कोसों दूर है। इन इलाकों में चेतना जगाने का कार्य अखबार से ज्यादा रेडियो और दूरदर्शन की पत्रकारिता कर सकती है। यहां बोले हुए शब्दों (दृश्य श्राव्य) का पहुंचना आसान है। इनके द्वारा लोगों के सोचने के तौर तरीके को बदलने से बड़ा कार्य हो सकता है ताकि लोग विकास की ओर उन्मुख हों। लोगों की सोच एवं व्यवहार में बदलाव आने पर ही वे विकास की ओर उन्मुख होंगें। इसमें सरकारी मशीनरी को ठीक राह पर चलाने की जरूरत है। उसकी बेरहमी या उदासीनता को पत्रकारिता द्वारा जनमत बनाकर दूर किया जा सकता है।

विकास की दृष्टि से अपेक्षित लक्ष्य की प्राप्ति की दिशा में आर्थिक–सामाजिक और राजनीतिक क्षेत्र के लोग भी महत्वपूर्ण रोल अदा कर सकते हैं लेकिन स्थानीय मीडिया का रोल सबसे अहं होता है। इसलिए आंचलिक भाषा में, स्थानीय प्रसार–तंत्र से विकास का संदेश पहुंचना ज्यादा उपयोगी हो सकता है। स्थानीय रेडियो केन्द्र, दूरदर्शन केन्द्र के साथ ही सामुदायिक अखबारों से ग्रामीण चेतना को रचनात्मक दिशा एवं गति दी जा सकती है। स्थानीय बोलियों एवं प्रयोगों का इसमें उपयोग जरूरी है। इससे उनमें ज्यादा जागृति आयेगी और विकास की गति भी तेज होगी।

ऐसे सामुदायिक पत्र को चलाना भी आज आसान नहीं है। एक तो वहां पहुंचना कठिन है दूसरे आज भी हमारे अधिकांश अखबार सरकारी विज्ञापन पर निर्भर रहते हैं। सरकार मदद करेगी तो वह उनकी नीतियों को भी प्रभावित करेगी। कई किस्म के दबाव काम करेंगे। इसलिए अखबार आर्थिक दृष्टि से आत्म–निर्भर हों, यह बड़ा पेचीदा सवाल है। ऐसे कार्य सामाजिक संगठन बखूबी कर सकते हैं। ऐसे अखबार निकल सकते हैं, जिनसे विकास के काम में मदद हो। विकास में लगी सरकारी मशीनरी पर जनमत का दबाव हो और शोषण के हिमायती या

संरक्षक स्थानीय दादाओं का शिकंजा ढीला पड़े। यह भी जरूरी है कि यह जागृति कोई गलत दिशा नहीं ले ले। कुछ इलाकों में विदेशी ताकतों द्वारा प्रेरित जागृति ने कुछ लोगों में देश के और उसकी अस्मिता, अखंडता एवं सांस्कृतिक धरोहर के ही खिलाफ नफरत के बीज बो दिए हैं। विघटनकारी एवं हिंसक तत्व भी जागृति के नाम पर सक्रिय हुए हैं। इस ओर ध्यान दिलाने का काम भी पत्रकारिता का है।

फिर भी हमारे अखबारों ने शासन और समाज का ध्यान ग्रामीण जीवन की ओर दिलाने तथा ग्रामीण चेतना जगाने में महत्वपूर्ण भूमिका अदा की है। ग्रामीण अंचल में बड़े नरसंहार या ज्यादती, बालकों की या महिलाओं की खरीद–फरोख्त, गंभीर बीमारियों के प्रकोप, जैसी कई खबरें ग्रामीण संवाददाताओं की जागरूकता का नतीजा है जिन पर पूरे देश का ध्यान गया। एक प्रमुख अंग्रेजी अखबार ने "हमारा गांव छतेरा" के शीर्षक कालम से ग्रामीण अंचल के जनजीवन एवं समस्याओं को अखबारों के माध्यम से प्रसारित करने में बड़ी भूमिका अदा की। इससे ग्रामीण अंचल की खबरों के प्रकाशन की होड़ पैदा हुई। पत्रकारिता एवं संचार का सीधा असर ग्रामीण परिवेश पर पड़ता है और इससे जागृति एवं बदलाव की गति तेज हुई है। उसे और भी सोद्देश्य सकारात्मक एवं रचनात्मक दिशा देने की जरूरत है।

अंत में सवाल यह उठता है कि क्या अखबारी जगत ग्रामीण जागृति के अनुरूप उस ओर ध्यान दे रहा है या कहीं कोई ढील है ?

मेरी राय में अनेक अखबार इस दिशा में सजग हैं और अपने उत्तरदायित्व का पूरी जिम्मेदारी से निर्वाह कर रहे हैं। इससे ग्रामीण अंचल में उन अखबारों का प्रसार भी बढ़ा है लेकिन कई अखबार और साप्ताहिक अभी इस दिशा में पूरी तरह सजग नहीं हैं। ग्रामीण अंचल की आवाज को स्वर देने की बजाय उनकी सुर्खियों में शहरी खबरें एवं राष्ट्रीय–अंतर्राष्ट्रीय घटनायें ज्यादा हावी रहती हैं। राजनीतिक घटनाक्रम या खींचतान ज्यादा जगह घेरता है। ग्रामीण अंचल की भावनायें, आवश्यकतायें, नये समय के अनुरूप उनके विकास के स्वर को स्वर देने के कार्य से अब अखबार नहीं बच सकते। उन्हे इस ओर ध्यान देना पड़ेगा वरना वे अप्रासांगिक बन जायेंगे। आने वाला समय आंचलिक पत्रकारिता का है। ग्रामीण आबादी की चेतना से कटकर अब अखबार अपनी स्थिति को मजबूत नहीं बना पायेंगे। समय के तकाजे को समझना आज की बड़ी जरूरत है। अब पुरानी रूढ़ियां टूट रही हैं। लोग आगे बढ़ने को उतावले हैं।

जो चेतना ग्रामीण क्षेत्रों में पैदा हो रही है, उसकी गति बड़ी तेज है। उसी गति से यदि शासन एवं समाज के सारे अंग नहीं चले तो फिर अव्यवस्था पैदा हो जायेगी। टकराव और हिंसा की घटनायें उसी अव्यवस्था की झलक है। अब

तो वनवासी और पहाड़ी अंचलों में भी चेतना आ रही है। अब उन्हें विकास की किरण एवं उनके अधिकारों से वंचित नहीं रखा जा सकता। इसे दिशा और दृष्टि देने से पत्रकारिता का रोल महत्त्वपूर्ण एवं उपयोगी है।

12

ग्रामीण महिलाओं के अधिकार व मीडिया का सहयोग

– इन्द्रा बिश्नोई

EMPOWERMENT OF RURAL WOMEN AND ROLE OF MEDIA

— Indira Bishnoi

Notwithstanding the fact that in India, legal and constitutional rights are already available, women suffer massive disadvantages in terms of basic needs and social equity. Women still form the most vulnerable section of the society. The successive five year plans placed special emphasis on providing health facilities, integrated with family welfare and nutrition, women's education, etc. It is, however, equally important to impart education to the rural women so that they could make use of information made available from the media. Economic development of rural areas would accelerate media development as well and the benefits would raise the level of social development and awareness of the rural population.

महिलाओं के अधिकारों के बारे में तरह–तरह की चर्चाएं और वार्ताएं समय समय पर होती रहती हैं तथा आज सरकार तथा अन्य स्वयंसेवी संस्थाएं भी इस बारे में जागरूक व चिंतित हैं कि ग्रामीण महिलाओं की स्थिति को कैसे सुधारा जाये व उन्हें समाज में बराबर का दर्जा दिलाया जाये। कानून व संविधान में तो महिलाओं के अधिकारों को सुरक्षित रखा गया है व संविधान में भी महिलाओं को पुरूषों के समान ही दर्जा व अधिकार दिये गये हैं व समान काम के लिए समान वेतन का भी प्रावधान है। लेकिन प्रश्न यह है कि इन संविधान प्रदत्त अधिकारों व सुरक्षा जो उसे प्रदान की गई है उसका पूरा लाभ उस तक पहुंचा है या नहीं। यह अपने

अधिकार जो उसे दिये गये हैं वह प्राप्त कर पाई है या नहीं। कुछ अधिकार या संरक्षण महिलाओं की स्थिति सुधारने के लिए किये गये हैं। उन संरक्षणों को महिलाओं को प्रदान करने व उनकी सामाजिक स्थिति में परिवर्तन लाने के लिए हमारी सरकार की जिम्मेदारियाँ हैं। जिन्हें पूरा करने के लिए वह अपनी विभिन्न योजनाएं बनाकर उसे अपने प्रशासनिक तेज के जरिये राज्य स्तर, जिला स्तर, ब्लाक स्तर व ग्राम स्तर पर लागू करती है। अब वह विभिन्न कल्याणकारी कार्यक्रमों को कैसे लागू करती है व उसके ऊपर किस प्रकार काम करती है यह उसका दायित्व है कि वह अपने नागरिकों की भलाई के लिए क्या विकासोन्मुख परियोजना बनाती है व किस प्रकार उसे कार्यान्वित करती है।

दूसरी महत्वपूर्ण बात यह है कि कुछ ऐसे महिलाओं के अधिकार हैं जो महिलाओं को स्वयं प्राप्त करने होते हैं। जब ऐसी परिस्थिति आ जाए जिसके द्वारा उसके अधिकारों को कुचला जाये या सामाजिक कोई ऐसी कुरीति या अव्यवस्था चल रही हो जिसके रहते उसके अधिकारों व सुरक्षा का हनन हो रहा हो तो वह उनकी रक्षा किया करे। जाहिर है कि वह अपने अधिकारों की रक्षा के लिए स्वयं जब तक संगठित होकर आगे नहीं आयेगी तब तक उसे सफलता नहीं मिलेगी। इसके लिए सबसे पहले उसे अपनी स्थिति, अहमियत, व्यक्तित्व व अधिकारों के बारे में जब तक पूरी जानकारी नहीं होगी तब तक वह इसमें सफल नहीं होगी। अब उसे अपने अधिकारों की जानकारी के लिए शिक्षा का होना बहुत जरूरी है। बगैर शिक्षा के उसे उसके अधिकारों, सामाजिक स्थिति व स्वयं की स्थिति के बारे में पता नहीं चलेगा और न ही यह पता चलेगा कि हमारे देश, दुनिया में पहले जो सामाजिक व्यवस्था व स्थिति थी उसमें क्या परिवर्तन पहले से अब हुए हैं। शिक्षा के द्वारा ही उसे विभिन्न संचार माध्यमों से उसे अपने आसपास की स्थिति व अन्य जगहों की स्थिति की तुलना करने में सहायता मिलेगी। शिक्षित होने से उसे देश में हो रही प्रगति का ज्ञान होगा व उस प्रगति का लाभ उठाने की उसकी इच्छा को बल मिलेगा व उसके मन में भी अपनी स्थिति सुधारने की इच्छा शक्ति पनपेगी। जब तक महिला के स्वयं के अन्दर जागरूकता पैदा नहीं होगी उसके कल्याण की संभावना कम ही है। अतः इसके लिए महिला का शिक्षित होना अति आवश्यक है।

आज हमारे शहरी क्षेत्रों की अपेक्षा गांवों में महिलाओं की स्थिति में कोई खास परिवर्तन नहीं आया है। इसका एक कारण नगरों में सब तरह की सुविधाओं व लोगों का शिक्षित होना है। हमारी अब तक की सरकारों ने ग्रामीण क्षेत्रों के विकास पर बहुत अधिक ध्यान न देने के कारण ही ऐसा हुआ है। एक तो दूरदराज के गांवों में लोगों का अशिक्षित होना व दूसरा उनके क्षेत्र में मूलभूत सुविधाओं जैसे कि सड़कें, बिजली, पानी की समुचित व्यवस्था न होना। जब एक

आम नागरिक इन्हीं सुविधाओं के अभाव में जीवनयापन करता है तो वह तो सिर्फ अपनी रोजीरोटी कमाने में ही अपना अधिकांश समय लगा देगा व दूसरी बातों की ओर उसका ध्यान ही नहीं जा सकेगा। इसलिए हम यह सोचें कि लोग अधिक से अधिक शिक्षित हों तो हमें पहले उन्हें मूलभूत सुविधाएं उपलब्ध करवानी चाहिएं ताकि वे अपनी आर्थिक स्थिति सुधार सकें। आर्थिक स्थिति के सुधरने पर ही वह शिक्षा की ओर सोच सकेगा। अपने बच्चों को शिक्षित करने के महत्व के बारे में सोच सकेगा। अतः हमें उसी वातावरण में रोजगार के ज्यादा से ज्यादा अवसर प्रदान करने चाहिए। यदि कोई व्यक्ति गांव में रहता है और उसके गांव में सड़क है जो उसे अन्य स्थान से जोड़ती है तो उसे दूसरी जगह जाकर व बाहर से लोगों को वहां लाकर कुछ उन्हें जानकारी उपलब्ध करवाने में आसानी होगी। कोई बाहर जाकर काम करेगा कोई बाहर से आकर उनसे काम करवाएगा। यदि वहां बिजली होगी तो उससे उनकी मुख्य आंय जोकि खेती है उसको बढ़ाने में सहायता मिलेगी। पीने का पानी उपलब्ध होगा तो उसे जो दूरदराज के क्षेत्रों से पीने का पानी लाने के लिए समय गंवाना पड़ता है उसमें बचत होगी व उस समय का सदुपयोग वह कर सकेगा। अब यदि सड़क है बिजली है तो उससे उसके गांव में रेडियो, टेलिविजन का आगमन होगा जिससे भी वह जागरूक होगा व उसे दुनिया में हो रही हलचल की जानकारी मिलती रहेगी नहीं तो वह सबसे कट कर एक ही ढर्रे पर जिंदगी जी रहा होगा। अगर उसका पुश्तैनी धंधा खेती है तो वह अब तक जैसा कि प्रकृति पर निर्भर रहता था वो नहीं होकर उसके बारे में जो अनुसंधान हुए हैं उसके बारे में जान सकेगा कि अगर पानी की कमी है तो कौन सी फसल बीजनी चाहिए, कब बोनी चाहिए व एक फसल के बाद कौन सी दूसरी फसल बोने से ज्यादा आमदनी हो सकती है यह सब उसे रेडियो, समाचार पत्र व दूरदर्शन से मालूम होगा। यह सब जब उसके इलाके में सड़क बिजली की सुविधा होगी तब प्राप्त होगा। इसके होने से उसकी आर्थिक स्थिति सुधरेगी। आर्थिक स्थिति से सम्पन्न होने पर वह शिक्षा की ओर ध्यान दे सकेगा व शिक्षित होने पर वह अपने अधिकारों के प्रति जागरूक होगा और यह जागरूकता उसे अपने अधिकार प्राप्त करने के लिए प्रेरित करेगी। जब वह इस ओर जागरूक होगा तब हमें यह कोशिश सरकार, संस्थाओं व संचार माध्यमों के द्वारा करनी होगी कि वह किस तरह से योजनाओं का, उपलब्ध साधनों का अधिक से अधिक लाभ कैसे उठा सके। इसके लिए सबसे महत्वपूर्ण मीडिया विभिन्न प्रकार के पत्रों, विभिन्न पारम्परिक लोक कलाओं इत्यादि द्वारा उन्हें जागृत किया जा सकता है।

इसके लिए ऐसे प्रकाशन जो विशेषकर ग्रामीण महिलाओं के लिए सरल भाषा, चित्रों इत्यादि के माध्यम से व विभिन्न सांस्कृतिक संस्थाओं द्वारा ऐसे कार्यक्रम

तैयार करें जो उनके समाज में व्याप्त कुरीतियों के कुप्रभावों बारे में बता सकें। अब तो चलते फिरते वाहनों में वीडियो फिल्म के द्वारा भी उन्हें जागृत किया जा सकता है। गांव में ऐसी गाड़ियां समयबद्ध कार्यक्रम के अनुसार जायें व महिलाओं की बेहतरी पर बने कार्यक्रमों की जानकारी दें। जिलाधिकारी ऐसे कार्यक्रम बनाएं जिनके द्वारा गांव–गांव में ऐसे केन्द्र स्थापित हों जो उनके लिए नियमित शिक्षा, स्वास्थ्य, सफाई इत्यादि के बारे में तो बतायें साथ–साथ उनको घर बैठे कुछ ऐसी चीजें बनाने की ट्रेनिंग दे जिसके लिए आवश्यक सामग्री वहीं उनके स्थान पर ही उपलब्ध हो जिसको कुछ अच्छा रूप देकर वे कलात्मक चीजों से अपना घर भी अच्छा करें व उनको कुछ आर्थिक सहायता भी मिल सके। जैसे गांव में मिट्टी के बर्तन बनाने वाला है उसे तरह–तरह के कलात्मक फूल लगाने वाले नये–नये डिजाइन के गमले इत्यादि बनाना सिखायें। कुछ ऐसी चीजें और गांवों में उपलब्ध होती हैं जिनसे जूट की तरह की दरियां, गलीचे, मूढ़े इत्यादि बनाने सिखाये जा सकते हैं। अतः सारांश यह है कि यदि हमें अपनी महिलाओं की स्थिति में विशेषकर ग्रामीण महिलाओं की स्थिति में सुधार लाना है तो –

१. उन्हे स्वयं को अपने अधिकार पाने के लिए जागरूक करना होगा।
२. उनके रहन–सहन व स्वास्थ्य के बारे में जानकारी उपलब्ध करवानी चाहिए ।
३. इसके लिए उन्हें प्रथम शिक्षा की व्यव्स्था करनी होगी।
४. उनकी आर्थिक स्थिति में परिवर्तन लाना होगा। उन्हें वहीं उनके आसपास के परिवेश में उपलब्ध चीजों को उपयोग में लाकर कुछ चीजें बनाने की ट्रेनिंग देकर, जिससे कि वे खुद कुछ कमा सकें घर बैठकर ही।
५. इस सबके लिए पहले उनके द्वारा चुनी गयी सरकार, उसके अधीन काम करने वाले अधिकारियों को एक ऐसा तंत्र तैयार करना पड़ेगा जिससे उनके क्षेत्र में मूलभूत सुविधाएं उन्हें मुहैया करवाई जायें जैसे सड़क, पानी, बिजली आदि।

इतना सब कुछ होने पर हम आशा कर सकते हैं कि अशिक्षा की वजह से हमारे समाज में जो रूढ़िवादी संस्कार व अंधविश्वास फैला हुआ है उसे दूर करने में हम कुछ हद तक सफल हो सकते हैं व रूढ़िवादिता व अंधविश्वास की दीवारें जब ढहने लग जायेंगी तब महिलाओं की जिन्दगी में खुशहाली रूपी रोशनी की किरणें पहुंचने लगेंगी और चूंकि महिलाएं समाज का महत्वपूर्ण अंग हैं अतः उनकी प्रगति के बिना समाज की सम्पूर्ण प्रगति संभव नहीं है।

ग्रामीण महिलाओं तक पहुंचने के लिए आंगनवाड़ी परियोजना बहुत ही लाभकारी है यदि यह जिस उद्देश्य को लेकर बनायी गयी है उसी के अनुरूप चल

सके। आंगनवाड़ी का उद्देश्य है कि किसी बच्चे की आरंभिक अवस्था में होने वाला शारीरिक, मानसिक और सामाजिक विकास उसके बाद के विकास के लिए निर्णायक होता है। इसलिए आरंभिक बाल अवस्था में विकास के दौरान उसे उपलब्ध करवाई गई सेवाएं बच्चे के विकास के लिए बहुत महत्त्वपूर्ण हैं। यह भी महसूस किया गया है कि बच्चे के उचित विकास के लिए पोषण, स्वास्थ्य और शिक्षा जैसी सभी आधारभूत जरूरी सेवाएं बच्चों और माताओं विशेषकर ग्रामीण क्षेत्र व शहरों की भी अविकसित व गरीब आबादी को एक साथ उनके अपने गांव या वार्ड में उपलब्ध करवायी जायें।

इस योजना के तहत माताओं को बच्चों के पोषण, उनके व उनके बच्चे के स्वास्थ्य के बारे में बताना व उनकी स्वास्थ्य जांच करना तथा स्कूल पूर्व शिक्षा आते हैं इससे पहले माँ को शिक्षा मिल जाती है व बच्चे की स्वास्थ्य सम्बन्धी प्राथमिक देखभाल भी हो जाती है। इसमें एक आंगनवाड़ी कार्यकर्ता होती है जो उस इलाके के करीब 1000 बच्चों की देखभाल करती है। यह कार्यकर्ता महिला होती है अतः ग्रामीण महिलाओं को भी समझाने में कठिनाई नहीं होती है व अधिकतर क्षेत्रों में वह उसी क्षेत्र की होती है जिनको कि ट्रेनिंग देकर इस लायक बनाया जाता है।

जब महिला शिक्षित होगी तो उसे कुछ पढ़ने की, कुछ जानने की, यदि बिजली है तो रेडियो सुनने की, दूरदर्शन देखने की लगन होगी क्योंकि शिक्षित होने की वजह से उसे कुछ समझ में आयेगा। शिक्षा की वजह से भी यह धारणा गांवों में है कि रेडियो, अखबार, दूरदर्शन ये सब आदमी के काम की चीजें हैं महिलाओं का इनसे कोई सरोकार नहीं जबकि सच्चाई यह है कि इन सब चीजों के प्रयोग करने का हक महिलाओं को भी उतना ही है जितना पुरूषों को। अशिक्षा की वजह से गांव में पर्दा प्रथा है जिसके रहते वे पुरूषों की उपस्थिति में यदि दूरदर्शन है तो भी नहीं देख पाती हैं। अतः जब तक ग्रामीणों में शिक्षा का स्तर, उनकी आर्थिक स्थिति नहीं सुधरेगी समाज के ढांचे में परिवर्तन संभव नहीं है और इसमें सबसे बड़ा रोल मीडिया का है जो यह निश्चित करे कि ग्रामीणों को किस प्रकार शिक्षित किया जाए व जो कुछ भी दुनियां में परिवर्तन हो रहे हैं उनकी जानकारी उन तक कैसे पहुंचे।

ANNEXURES

ANNEXURE I

I. RECOMMENDATIONS ON EDITING A RURAL NEWSPAPER

The recommendations broadly involved four areas :

* Editorial policy and functions
* Personnel and training
* Sources
* Feedback mechanism and readership survey

1. Editorial Policy and Functions

Objectives The group stressed the need for the paper's thrust to be local in character. National and international events would receive coverage dependent on their relevance to the population. The accent should be on providing news which had use. At the same time, the function of the paper was to inform, educate, make the rural audience aware, ensure their involvement and participation and provide a forum for redressing grievances.

Functions It would do the above through reports, features, letters to the editors. Rather than have editorials which the Group felt might be interpreted by a rural audience as being 'talked' down to, a 'your opinion' 'our opinion' column would be both interactive and comment oriented. The group also emphasised the need for pictorial visibility, bearing in mind the literacy levels of the audience profile.

Periodicity The group felt the frequency of the newspaper was an issue which should be discussed alongwith the management. However, the periodicity would be primarily determined by newsflow, infrastructural facilities like manpower and equipment and audience demand.

Reach	The newspaper should reach as many members of the community at all levels.
Language	Local and written in a conversational style which could be easily understood by most of the readers.
Editorial advertise-ment space	This again would warrant a discussion with the management. But broadly speaking, two options emerged during the group discussions. *Option 1* : To work towards sponsorship from industry. This, however, was often not possible. Consequently, most of the group evinced reservations about using such a strategy on a regular basis. *Option 2 :* Contrary to the current trends in main-stream urban newspapers where editorial space was often determined in accordance with the quantum of advertisements generated, the group felt a pre-determined editorial–advertisement ratio was desirable. This should be at least 60 per cent in favour of news/editorial space. The group also voiced that preference should be given to public and community service advertisements like social hygiene and rural health.

2. Personnel and Training

The Group felt that the catchword here was undisputably on professionalism. And so while on 'insider approach' was desirable in so far as they would have direct participation, access and understanding of their rural environment, training should be professional and conducted by experts. In this context, the rural press could have tie ups/associations with individual journalists who had worked in the mainstream press, journalism schools, and other professional institutes like RIND, PIIX, UNESCO, and other relevant rural development agencies and organizations.

An apprenticeship training programme was also suggested once the paper became established.

As far as training methodology at the local level was concerned, the emphasis should be on practical workshops. While experience, insight and local orientation all came into play in the selection personnel, the group also highlighted the need for language skills, sensitivity and awareness of current local issues.

Recruitment could give particular attention to the following areas : NGOs, youth and organisations actively involved in local issues.

3. Sources The news sources could broadly be divided into two categories: (a) sources within and (b) sources without.

(a) *Sources within :* Community taluk office, panchayat, government bodies like police, collectors office, etc. Another vital source was NGOs working within the community. The journalists should also maintain contact with the local MPs and MLAs. However, this should in no way jeopardise the autonomy of the paper.

(b) *Outside sources :* Research institutes doing work which could be related to the local environment. The journalists would also maintain regular contact with correspondents of mainstream newspapers. Contact would also be maintained with state govt. departments and projects. These would be regularly monitored and status of programmes relevant to the community would be reported.

4. Feedback This was vital to ensure that the paper served as an accurate pulse of the community. Feedback would be developed through :

(a) Inter-personal communication between reporters and the community.

(b) Follow up action on specific issues which were vital to the community.

(c) A regular 'letters to the editor' column would be published and given due weightage.

Ashish Sen
Chairman : Group I

ANNEXURE II

RECOMMENDATIONS ON MANAGEMENT OF A RURAL NEWSPAPER

The group which discussed the management aspects of a rural newspaper made the following recommendations.

1. Although the problems of rural press and particularly the journalist were identified, the group felt that the need and prospects for rural press were justified.
2. The availability of improved telecommunications and numerous options for producing a newspaper had enhanced the potential of bringing out a newspaper.
3. The question of finance loomed large in the minds of the members. They all felt that banking institutions with significant clientele in the rural areas could be approached. The proposed newspaper development corporation may facilitate availability of finance. Further, qualified graduates, especially women, could approach entrepreneurship development corporations for finance. Institutions such as RIND had already explored certain mechanisms for these ventures. The idea of approaching individuals did not receive much encouragement. With some reservations, it was suggested that members of parliament could be approached to consider funding rural newspapers from the newly created constituency development fund.
4. Since there was no specific procedure for starting a rural newspaper, the group recommended adoption of the existing rules and regulations. The experience of different associations for small and medium newspapers particularly language newspapers is useful.
5. Mr. Rajeshwar Dyal specifically mentioned that a number of national and international funding agencies interested in

development could consider good proposals for starting a newspaper(s).

6. The group felt that there should not be any compromise on production features. Since technology was available for bringing out small newspapers and publications, they should be used.
7. Motivated group of people is needed for such venture. Experienced and retired journalists who have returned to their native towns and villages can be hired to lend professional expertise in design and layout. Once the venture gets going the second line can move in. Using the services of correspondents and stringers of the mainstream papers was not recommended as it would lead to the very same problems that formed the basis of organization of the AMIC seminar.
8. The newspaper should be priced. However, as a promotional venture, this priced publication can be distributed free from a few months or maximum one year. This would give the readers an idea of the publication.
9. Advertising revenue for the newspaper was considered as bright. Due to liberalisation and expansion of the market base, advertisers are willing to incorporate rural newspapers into their media planning. R.V. Rajan endorsed this vision based on his reading of the situation as an advertising and marketing executive. The audience recommended that big companies might support the venture as a goodwill gesture.
10. The rural newspaper can become a companion medium of the broadcast media and thereby supplement the developmental efforts of electronic media. Grassroot workers of various NGOs could be used as correspondents for the newspaper. With some training unemployed youth in the villages could also be used.

B. P. Sanjay
Chairman Group II

ANNEXURE III

MANAGEMENT OF RURAL NEWSPAPERS

1. Rural newspapers must have a communication package which is not co-terminus with the packages of the city-based newspapers. Intra-party or inter-party politics, detailed reports on cricket, the columns of the Indo-Pak tussle at the Human Rights Conference in Geneva, are of interest to city-dwellers, but the vast majority of the rural audience cannot be interested in the "how" and "why", only in a gist of "what" happened.
2. The communication package of rural newspapers must concentrate on community service. It must report about new kinds of fertilisers, new trains to the nearest railway station, a boy or girl from the catchment area of the rural community getting a doctorate or a posh job in Delhi or Calcutta, whose son is getting married to whose daughter, etc.
3. Non-local news should be confined to a small part (say a fourth) of the issue. Much of it can come from AIR's slow-speed bulletins. Recycling important bits of news from nearby big-city newspaper is also all right, provided it is condensed to be palatable to its readership.
4. News gathering and distribution of the printed copies of the paper have to be largely honorary.

   Even for big newspapers the bulk of the primary news comes from part-time correspondents or stringers. The Bhagalpur blindings were first reported by a stringer. The inundation of a district town in Uttar Pradesh was also first reported by a stringer of the daily *Aaj* who swam and waded through flood waters to reach the nearest telegraph office just to telegraph the news. Most eloquently, AIR in its next news bulletin quoted the *Aaj* stringer as the source to report that the town was submerged in flood waters rushing in after bursting the protective embankment.

5. Honorary correspondentship is not a rare phenomenon. The bulk of the primary news, even in city-based newspapers, comes from part-time or honorary correspondents.

   Part-time or honorary correspondentship may not give money. But it gives clout, prestige and status to the correspondent.

   In rural newspapers this has more of a prospect. For rural people as a rule do not hanker after money, they are happy with the prestige and status that it brings.

6. The strategy has to be to enlarge the catchment area of rural newspapers to embrace more and more villages. If this is done, the clout and therefore the viability of the newspaper will increase.

To Sum up

(a) The rural newspaper is, and should be, a community service, giving news of immediate interest to the particular rural community. Such news is hot news for members of the community but is usually considered non-news by city-based papers. For non-community news, radio slow-speed and other bulletins are a good source.

(b) The news gathering and distribution have largely to be honorary. A hawker system is unlikely to be successful. A better, if unorthodox, distribution system would be to put copies of the paper at the village grocery or other place where people routinely and frequently go.

(c) The honorary news gathering system has a proven track record even in city-based journalism. Much of the time first news of an event or happening is broken by stringers, who are part-time correspondents and work not for the money but for the prestige, clout and satisfaction.

(d) Financing has to be unorthodox and based on community service and community feeling.

    Advertisements will be sparse to begin with. The strategy is to go on expanding the catchment area for news gathering and circulation and to include the nearby town, railway station, weekly *hat,* etc. If this can be done, advertisers will find it difficult to ignore rural newspapers.

Indian Institute of Mass
Communication—Dhenkanal

LIST OF CONTRIBUTORS

Vir Bala Aggarwal, Assistant Professor, Department of Journalism and Mass Communication, Himachal Pradesh University, Shimla.

Anjan Kumar Banerji *Padamshri* Professor Emeritus, Department of Journalism, Banaras Hindu University, Varanasi.

Sanjeev Bhanawat, Incharge, Communication Centre, Rajasthan University, Jaipur.

Indira Bishnoi, Social Activist, associated with several grassroot organizations and educational institutions, Fatehbad, Haryana.

Ashok Chaturvedi, Editor, Amarjyoti News and Features Agency (ANFA) and President, Rural Journalists Association of India, Jaipur.

V. S. Gupta, Professor, Directorate of Publications, Haryana Agricultural University, Hisar.

G. P. Jain, Journalist and Social Worker, New Delhi.

K. S. Ramakrishnan, Director, Research Institute for Newspaper Development, Madras.

B. P. Sanjay, Professor and Head, Department of Communication, Manonmaniam Sundarnar University, Tirunelveli.

Radhey Shyam Sharma, Director General, Makhanlal Chaturvedi National University of Journalism, Bhopal.

A.K. Varma, Professor, Indian Institute of Mass Communication, Dhenkanal.

J. S. Yadava, Director, Indian Institute of Mass Communication, New Delhi.

BIBLIOGRAPHY

Agarwal, Narendra (1977). Agricultural reporting in India — A brief overview. *Media Asia,* 4(1/2): 25-27.

Arbind, K. Sinha (1987). *Mass Media and Rural Development : A Study of Village Communication in Bihar,* New Delhi.

Berriegan, Frances J. (1977). A manual on mass media in population and development. UNESCO.

Bhagat Rekha and Mathur, P.N. (1989). *Mass Media and Farm Women.* New Delhi: Intellectual Publishing House.

Braid, F. R. (1993). Communication and Development in the New Asian Context. *AMCB,* 23(4): 10-11.

Dogra, Bharat (1984). The Realities of Rural Reporting. *Vidura.*

Dua, M. R. and V. S. Gupta (eds.) (1994). *Media and Development.* New Delhi: Har Anand Publications.

Dutt, R. C. (1990). Rural Development—Some Reflections. *Yojana,* 34 (14 & 15) : 5-8.

Etienne, Gilbert (1985). *Rural Development in Asia. Meetings with Peasants,* New Delhi: Sage.

FAO (1987a). *The Paradigm of Communication in Development.* From knowledge transfer to community participation—Lessons from the Grameen Bank, Bangladesh Development Communication—A Case Study, Rome.

FAO (1987b). *Development Support Communication.* Expert Consultation, Rome.

Gupta, V. S. (1979). Development Communication — An Emerging Concept, *Vidura,* 16 (3) : 197-199.

Gupta, V. S. (1981). Communication Planning — A plea for appropriate communication. *Media Asia,* 8(3) : 156-161.

— (1987). Rural press development in India — Status, factors affecting its growth and future prospects. *Media Asia,* 14(2) : 67-72.

— (1989a). *Rural Press : Problems and Prospects.* New Delhi : Press Institute of India.

— and Ranjit Singh (1994). *Communication Planning for Socio-Economic Development.* New Delhi : Har Anand Publications.

— (1995). Rural Development and Media Strategies and *Third Revolution in Indian Perspective : Contemporary issues and themes in Communication.* New Delhi : Concept Publishing Company.

Guy, de Fontgalland (ed.) (1976. *AMIC Study Seminar on Development Communication, March 1985—A Report.* AMIC : Singapore.

Habermann, Pater and Guy de Fontgalland (1978). Development Communication. AMIC, Singapore.

IARI (1980). Agricultural Journalism and Rural Development, in : *Research in Extension Education—Some basic findings,* New Delhi.

Jain, G. P. (1979). Rural Press. *Seminar* No. 235 : 23-25, New Delhi.

Khan, A. W. (1979). Better information through radio for small farmers, New Delhi. *Communicator*, 14(3) : 47-49.

Kothari, Rajni (1981). Publishing for Rural India, in : *Publishing for Rural Areas in Developing Countries.* New Delhi : National Book Trust.

Kuppuswamy, B. (1976). *Communication and Social Development in India.* New Delhi : Sterling Publishers Pvt. Ltd.

Melkote, Srinivas R. (1991). *Communication for Development in the Third World — Theory and Practice.* New Delhi : Sage.

Mody, Bella (1991). *Designing Messages for Development Communication.* New Delhi : Sage.

Nair, K. S. and S. A. White (1993). *Perspective on Development Communication.* New Delhi : Sage.

Nair, L. R. (1967). Private Press in National Development : The Indian Example in Lerner, Daniel and Wilbur Schramm (eds.) *Communication and Change in the Developing Countries.* Honolulu: East West Centre Press.

Rogers, Everett, M. (1976). Communication and Development. The Passing of the Dominant Paradigm in : Rogers Everett M. (ed.), *Communication and Development, Critical Perspectives,* Newbury Park. C. A.: Sage.

Schramm, Wilbur (1964). *Mass Media and National Development.* Stanford University Press, USA.

Swaminathan, M. S. (1973). *Our Agricultural Future.* Sardar Patel Memorial Lectures. New Delhi : All India Radio.

UNESCO (1982). *Many Voices, One World.* The International Commission on the Study of Communication Problems.

UNESCO (1986). IPDC News, No. 8.

Ward, W. B. (1971). Mass Media in India's Agricultural Development. *Vidura,* 5.

Yadava, J. S. (1994). Communication and Development—The Indian Experience, in Dua, M. R. and Gupta, V. S. (eds.), *Media and Development.* New Delhi : Har Anand Publications.

INDEX